MORE PROJECTS
FROM PINE

33 New Plans for the Beginning Woodworker

James A. Jacobson

TAB BOOKS Inc.
Blue Ridge Summit, PA

Dedication

To Ann F. Jacobson and Helen M. Park,
My designers and tracers,
With thanks and love

FIRST EDITION
SECOND PRINTING

Copyright © 1988 by James A. Jacobson
Printed in the United States of America

Library of Congress Cataloging in Publication Data

Jacobson, James A.
More projects from pine.

Bibliography: p.
Includes index.
1. Woodwork.   2. Pine.   I. Title.
TT180.J27   1988   684'.08   88-2246
ISBN 0-8306-0171-6
ISBN 0-8306-2971-8 (pbk.)

TAB BOOKS Inc. offers software for
sale. For information and a catalog,
please contact TAB Software Department,
Blue Ridge Summit, PA 17294-0850.

Questions regarding the content of this book
should be addressed to:

Reader Inquiry Branch
TAB BOOKS Inc.
Blue Ridge Summit, PA 17294-0214

Contents

4 Finishing and Hanging Projects **161**

Reasons for Finishing — Preliminaries to Finishing — Types of Finishes—Finishing Procedures—Hanging Devices and Procedures

Acknowledgments

I wish to thank the following companies for providing photographs and granting permission to use them:

Adjustable Clamp Co., Chicago, IL
Borden, Inc., Columbus, OH
Campbell-Hausfeld Co., Harrison, OH
Delta International Machinery Corp., Pittsburgh, PA
Dremel, Division of Emerson Electric Co., Racine, WI
Enco Manufacturing Co., Chicago, IL
Leichtung, Inc., Cleveland, OH
Northwestern Steel and Wire Co., Sterling, IL
Porter-Cable Corp., Jackson, TN
Red Devil, Inc., Union, NJ
Senco Products, Inc., Cincinnati, OH
Stanley Tools, Division of the Stanley Works, New Britain, CT
Warren Tool Co., Rhineback, NY
Woodworks, Ft. Worth, TX
Vermont American Tool Co., Division of Vermont American, Lincolnton, NC

Special acknowledgment and thanks are extended to Peter J. Jacobson for doing all the photographic work for the manuscript and the initial cover design.

Introduction

In recent years, there has been an increasing interest in do-it-yourself projects. For a variety of reasons, including economics, most of us prefer to do as many things around the house as possible. These projects not only are worth doing in themselves, they also provide a vehicle for the constructive use of our leisure time. Although many of these do-it-yourself projects are a combination of satisfaction and frustration, few result in lifelong hobbies. The intention of do-it-yourself projects is to get something done rather quickly with a minimum of investment and, hopefully, some success and a large degree of satisfaction.

Over the years, I have observed an interest and fascination on the part of many persons to do some woodworking. This interest seems to focus not on complex pieces of furniture, but rather on more mundane items, such as shelves, towel hangers, mirrors, and decorative pieces to hang on the walls. This book seeks to meet this interest by providing a series of projects that can be made from pine.

In addition to presenting projects that can be readily made by the nonwoodworker, this book gives suggestions for those who want to make these designs in quantity to sell at craft shows. Although production work requires some of the larger floor tools, the projects in this book all can be made in quantity with relative ease.

The projects presented also permit the homeowner, student, or production woodworker to make pieces that are generally considered "country." In recent years, there has been a national love affair with those things that represent a life-style different from our own. This is exemplified by the extensive and intensive interest in things that are both Early American and Country in theme. Making your own country projects will give the various pieces an authenticity not found in purchased items. Making your own decorative and functional accessories places you in the mainstream of true American crafting.

Although the projects do not require any decorative embellishments, they can be enhanced through a diversity of methods. Most of the projects are designed to present sufficient surface for tole painting. If you are actively engaged in tole painting, you will find that, with a minimum of effort, you also can make your own projects for painting. Since tole painting is not an area of expertise for me, I have included a Bibliography to assist you in developing skills in this area. Woodburning and carving are two other methods that can be used to enhance the various projects. Pine is an ideal wood to use for either carving or whittling, along with woodburning, to make more attractive pieces.

Another important emphasis in this book is original design. Suggestions and methods are provided to assist you in designing your own projects. The various projects are designed to help you develop confidence in your own abilities. Although you might approach the various tasks as do-it-yourself projects, you might very well end up as a captive to the design and woodworking process.

It is the intention of this book to help you build, finish, and hang, if needed, the various projects you decide are needed in your house. You can make the projects as presented, or redesign them to meet a specific need. In many of the projects, possible optional design considerations are presented.

To make your crafting easier and more informed, information on pine and the selection of lumber for projects is presented in detail. Information and suggestions on tools and their various accessories also are given to assist you in both planning and doing the projects. Following the project chapter, a final section details the finishing process from beginning to end. It also includes such necessary information as ways to hang a shelf. Sources for specialty items, such as Shaker pegs and candle holders, and a range of other items, such as tools, are listed as an Appendix. To assist you in becoming a more informed woodworker and to provide specialized information, an extensive Bibliography is provided.

Chapter 1

Wood for Projects

Although woodworking can be immensely practical and satisfying, it is the wood itself that makes it all possible. Wood, as you might know, can be an endless source of fascination and pleasure. It is one of those wonderous phenomena of nature that never ceases to interest and fascinate most people. You will discover, as you become involved in woodworking, that much of the pleasure is in learning about the different woods that are available.

Added to this learning process is the very challenging experience of selecting your boards for a particular project. All wood, even a seemingly worthless piece, presents you with an interesting decision-making process as you examine it in relation to a possible project. In many instances, you will discover that the wood you are examining will suggest an object or a project. Before you can explore the process of selecting wood for a particular project, you will need to have some information about wood in general.

WOOD

Basically, there are two primary groups of wood: the hardwoods and the softwoods. Interestingly enough, these designations have nothing to do with the actual hardness or softness of the wood itself. In fact, some hardwoods are quite soft, while a number of softwoods are rather hard. For example, most wood-carvers prefer working with basswood because it is a very soft wood with a uniform grain. It is easy to carve and is soft enough that a fingernail will readily penetrate its surface. Basswood, however, is designated as a hardwood. The designations of hardwood and softwood have, over a period of years, been generally accepted as representing the two primary categories of wood.

The actual distinctions between woods are, in fact, based on a number of rather technical factors. For example, the type of cell structure in the wood itself is one way of distinguishing between hardwoods and softwoods. The details of cell structure in wood is a very technical area. The Bibliography lists a number of reference books on the subject. You will find other references that will assist you in exploring the fascinating area of the technology of wood. For our purposes, it is sufficient to know that hardwoods and softwoods can be identified rather accurately and easily by their leaves. For example, trees with broad leaves, such as oak, birch, maple, cherry, walnut, hickory, and elm, are generally considered hardwoods. They generally shed their leaves in the fall, and so are called *deciduous*. Trees with needles, such as pine, spruce fir, and other evergreens, are called *conifers,* and are generally classified as softwoods. Another characteristic that distinguishes woods is the amount of sap, or *resin,* they contain. Softwoods generally contain substantial amounts of resin. You also will discover a very real difference between the woods in the marketplace: hardwoods are expensive, softwoods are not.

LEARNING ABOUT WOOD

Although the softwoods, pine in particular, will be the primary wood recommended for most projects, you should begin to become more informed on all the woods. Many books on wood are available for purchase or loan from your local library. Additionally, numerous government publications deal with the technology of wood. A number of references are provided in the Bibliography.

Another source of learning is the craft fairs that almost every community seems to have during the summer. Most people in wood crafts are delighted to share information about woods, their use, sources of supply, and other helpful information. You also might find yourself gleaning a few ideas for projects. I urge you to patronize these local craftsmen.

A final, and probably more exciting, source of learning about woods is your local lumber or hardwood dealer. Most lumberyards stock primarily softwoods because their customers are usually contractors, homebuilders, and homeowners. They can be very helpful when you go to purchase your material or ask questions. Be careful, however, not to assume that just because they sell lumber they also know about it. If you have done your homework, in many instances you will be better informed than the employees.

You also might want to locate a hardwood dealer in your area or, if available, a hardwood sawmill. In most instances, hardwood dealers are delighted to spend time answering what seems to you to be a "dumb" question. They not only will help you learn the names and characteristics of the different hardwoods, but they might explain the various grading and measuring systems used. Most dealers, for example, will explain the difference between kiln-dried (KD) and air-dried (AD) lumber. They probably will show you how the different methods of sawing a log—for example, plain sawing, rift sawing, and quartersawing—affect the way a board looks and its potential use. Seek out the individuals in your area who work with wood and are clearly knowledgeable about it. This kind of information can be a great asset in planning and initiating a range of projects around the house.

PINE: THE RIDICULED WOOD

With few exceptions, I have crafted with most of the common hardwoods and continue to do so on a regular basis. Certain items I craft simply look better and are generally supposed to be made from hardwoods. When I want to build a shelf for my house, however, I always turn to my pile of pine. Pine is unquestionably the wood of choice for home accessories.

For crafting accessories, I normally buy pine that is readily available at my local lumberyard. As a rule, I buy the least expensive grade, but I select the boards very carefully. I do not use what generally is called *yellow pine*. It tends to split and sliver, normally has very few knots, and is simply a rather drab, unexciting wood. You might want to avoid using it for your projects.

Actually, pine is a rather incredible wood. Shortly, I will provide you with specifics on how to buy it. First, however, I would like to defend this much maligned and ridiculed phenomenon frequently referred to as "It's only pine." Unlike the hardwoods, almost every piece of pine seems to be different. Its grains are unpredictable, and thus fascinating to examine. Pine has large and small, round and oblong knots that are sheer wonderments of detail. It frequently will have a certain red, grey, or brownish hue as a result of minerals taken in with water through the root system. You can drive a nail into pine without first drilling a hole. It lends itself to every conceivable type of finish. It smells good and clean, and normally will not make the user sneeze or have an allergic reaction. You literally can make anything out of pine. When you make a serious mistake and ruin a piece, you might have lost some time and effort, but not too much money in material. Also, you frequently can reuse your mistakes. If you are inclined to throwing things in the shop when you become angry or frustrated, pine will not do too much damage to the wall. You can hang an item made of pine on a wall without needing to secure it to studs. Pine cuts well, sands easily, and will hold together with almost any type of glue. In order to get hardwood logs to burn in a fireplace or woodburner, you must start the fire with pine or another softwood. Those who demean this multipurpose wonder of nature are either generally uninformed about wood or are simply snobs. Never apologize for using pine in your projects. Without it, there would be no houses in which to place your projects.

SELECTING PINE FOR PROJECTS

Unlike many other items you purchase, lumber has had a somewhat uniform grading system for many years. Although there remain some inconsistencies, standards regarding the varying qualities of lumber have been in place for many years. There are systems of grading or evaluating both the hardwoods and the softwoods. Each system is different, and each has its own unique symbols and language for varying degrees of quality. The grade a particular board is assigned by a lumber grader generally will determine the final cost to the consumer. As with buying meat or eggs, it can be important to have some working knowledge of lumber grading systems.

Because the focus of this book is pine, it will be important for you to know how pine is graded when you select material for your projects. The following information represents a rather crude compilation of softwood grading and the meaning of the various letters and numbers stamped on boards. References that include more scientifically detailed systems for grading lumber, including hardwoods, are included in the Bibliography.

Select Lumber

Boards that are classified as Select normally are almost perfectly clear, usually with no knots or other visible flaws in the board. There are generally four grades of select lumber, which are simply identified as: grades A, B, C, and D. It is very hard for the average person to distinguish between the various grades. Grade A would be defined as the perfect board, while Grade D would have some visible flaws. Grades B and C would fall somewhere between these two extremes. Generally, most Select boards are used for flooring, paneling, finishing, cabinetwork, and trim. As you might guess, Select grades are very expensive and frequently difficult to obtain.

Common Lumber

The second major classification of the softwoods is generally called Common. A board that is graded as Common has too many flaws, knots, or other defects for it is to be used for cabinetwork or trim. Boards classified as Common are further broken down by a numbering system.

No. 1. A board that is graded No. 1 Common is usually a rather choice piece. It often will be an almost totally clear board with a few small, but tight, knots. There are seldom any visible signs of sap or mineral coloration. No. 1 generally should have no warps, splits, twists, or decay. These types of flaws are presented in more detail shortly. As a rule, No. 1 is far too expensive for crafting projects. Although cost discourages its use, I also do not buy it because it lacks character. As with the Select grades, it is almost sterile in appearance.

No. 2. As you might guess, No. 2 Common is almost as good as No. 1, but might have some loose knots, a few checks on the end of the board, or some mineral staining. If you are not a lumber grader, I suspect you must take the word of the dealer that a board has been graded No. 2 Common. I have yet to see No. 2 Common in a lumberyard. It really does not seem to be available but, if it does exist, I suspect it is rather expensive.

No. 3. No. 3 Common is generally described as a medium-quality board to be used for general construction. It is often quite knotty and has visible defects, such as mineral discolorations. There are occasional checks, rotting and other strange-looking things that you have never seen before in a board. In this grade, a portion of the board often is not usable because of a split or warp. Despite, and yet because of, all that is wrong with No. 3 Common, I view it as the primary medium for the craftsman. To sort through a stack of No. 3 Common is always an exciting experience. The growth process of the tree, its multiple encounters with the elements, and the sheer beauty of a piece of wood confront you as you examine each board. I have found the multiple stacks of No. 3 Common to be almost a natural art gallery—an aesthetic encounter that can be experienced only via some wonderous phenomenon of nature. If you are less inclined to the beauty of the material, remember that No. 3 Common is also considerably less expensive than the other grades.

No. 4. No. 4 Common is generally made up of boards that have large knotholes and substantial splits, and is almost useless other than for general construction work. Do not rule this grade out entirely, though. If it is available, you frequently can find enough material for small projects. As you would suspect, this grade should be less expensive than the previous grade.

No. 5. No. 5 is generally considered to be scrap or waste lumber. I have frequently seen what looks like No. 5 Common, but that has been priced and called No. 3 Common. I cannot ever recall having seen a stack of No. 5 Common in a lumberyard.

As indicated earlier, the foregoing is but a crude and somewhat personal detailing of a rather sophisticated and scientifically based process. To date, it has been adequate to meet my informational needs when buying pine for projects. I would urge you, however, to explore the grading system in more detail as your interest in woodworking develops.

DIMENSIONS AND PRICING OF PINE

In addition to some notion about the grading of softwoods, you also need to realize that the actual width of a board is never the same as its referenced width. The length is almost always accurate. It is the width, unfortunately the thickness too, that gets confusing and requires a bit of memory work.

When boards are cut from a log at the sawmill, they are *rough-cut*. They do not have the smooth finish of the boards you buy at the lumberyard. The sawing process leaves all surfaces and edges of the board very rough. Rough, unplaned boards always should measure exactly the dimensions stated. For example, a rough, unplaned 1-×-4-inch board should measure exactly 1 inch

× 4 inches. This measurement is referred to as its *nominal size.*. The lumber you buy is always planed and will not be the exact, or nominal, dimensions that it is called. A 1-×-4-inch rough board, after planing, will be ¾ inch × 3½ inches. Table 1-1 presents the nominal (rough-cut) and the true (planed) sizes of wood that you will be buying at a lumberyard. It is important to remember these actual dimensions of the stock when you are planning and laying out your projects.

Although the various board sizes listed in Table 1-1 are all-inclusive, they represent the sizes that will be used in the projects in this book. If you commit some of the true dimensions to memory, you will greatly simplify your selection of material at the lumberyard. After awhile, however, you will know the various board sizes simply by looking at them.

Familiarity with the various widths also can be helpful when the lumberyard has a limited inventory. For example, if you need 1-×-4 stock for a given project and it is not available, you can always buy 1-×-8 stock and ripsaw it. This is not only an efficient way to obtain the needed stock, but it is often economical.

As well as having some knowledge of lumber dimensions and grading before you go to purchase your material, you should have some notion of how lumber prices are figured. Depending upon where you purchase your wood, one of two methods of pricing is generally used. Some lumber dealers sell boards by the *lineal foot.* A lineal foot is literally 12 inches long. The price of a board varies in relation to the width. Thus, a 1-×-4-inch board that is 5 feet long would cost a designated amount based on the lineal-foot price. A 1-×-6-inch board that is 5 feet long would cost more because the lineal-foot price would be higher for a wider board. You probably will discover that dealers who price lumber using this method often have considerably higher prices than those who deal in volume and use a different pricing method. On occasion, however, you might only need one board and will find that buying it at a store which sells by the lineal foot is quick and easy.

Table 1-1. Dimensions of Lumber.

THICKNESS AND WIDTH (Examples)	
Nominal Size (Rough Cut)	True Size (Planed)
1" × 4"	¾" × 3 ½"
1" × 6"	¾" × 5 ½"
1" × 8"	¾" × 7 ¼"
1" × 10"	¾" × 9 ¼"
1" × 12"	¾" × 11 ¼"
2" × 4"	1 ½" × 3 ½"
2" × 6"	1 ½" × 5 ½"
2" × 8"	1 ½" × 7 ¼"

Lumber dealers or distributors normally sell lumber by the *board foot*. A board foot of lumber is equal to the width (in inches) times the thickness (in inches) times the length (in feet) divided by 12. A simpler definition is that a board foot is 1 square foot of lumber that is 1 inch thick. Incidentally, when measuring the board to compute its cost, the lumber dealer uses the nominal size and not the true size of the board. The cost of having the board planed is figured into the board-foot price. An example of how to figure the board feet in a piece of pine lumber follows:

Board to be purchased is: 1″ (thick) × 6″ (wide) × 12′ (long)

$$\frac{\text{Thickness (inches)} \times \text{Width (inches)} \times \text{Length (feet)}}{12} = 1 \text{ board foot}$$

$$\frac{1″ \text{ (thickness)} \times 6″ \text{ (width)} \times 6′ \text{ (length)}}{12} = \frac{72}{12} = 6 \text{ board feet}$$

After making these calculations, the lumber dealer would check the current price per board foot for the grade and dimensions of the board selected. Because lumber dealers and their suppliers deal in terms of thousands of board feet, the prices are calculated in the thousands. To take the example one step further, your lumber dealer will tell you that your 1-×-6 board that is 12 feet long will cost $.2760 per board foot. Since you know you have 12 board feet in your piece of lumber, simple multiplication will tell you the cost of the board.

$$
\begin{array}{rl}
\$\ \ .2760 & \text{price per board foot} \\
\times \quad \ 12 & \text{number of board feet in } 1″ \times 6″ \times 12′ \text{ piece} \\
\hline
\$\ 3.31 & \text{the cost of your board}
\end{array}
$$

Although all these measurements and calculations are done for you at the lumberyard, you should be knowledgeable about the process. More often than not, you will find yourself selecting boards based on project need and appearance, rather than board feet. As you will discover the more you engage in woodworking, inches and fractions of an inch will be the kind of measuring in which you will need to develop some skill.

SHOPPING FOR PINE

Because you should have sufficient background information about lumber, I will address the actual shopping process for wood. Obviously, before you start for the lumberyard, you should have some idea of what you are going to make. You can focus or even accelerate this decision by reviewing, in detail, some of the projects in this book. Let us assume, for purposes of discussion, that you have decided to make the Single Towel Bar with Shelf. After measuring the area where you plan to hang the shelf, you decide it should be 20 inches long and at least 5 inches wide. Following some pencil and paper work with your design, patterns, and ruler, you decide you will need a 1-×-6 board that is 6 feet long. Let us further assume that you will purchase your lumber at your local lumberyard.

On occasion as you enter the world of a lumber dealer, you will find yourself being "helped" by someone who assumes you are stupid. I suspect this situation might be especially true for women entering this traditionally male domain. In addition to having good information about the material you want, you should bring along a tape measure. Indicate to the person waiting on you what you need and that you would like to select the material yourself. Some lumberyards discourage customers from entering areas where personal injury could result. Frequently, however, they will permit access to the lumber storage areas if you are accompanied by an employee.

Lumber is usually stacked according to grade, width, and length. Hopefully, an employee will lead you to an area where you will see stacks of 1 × 4s, 1 × 6s, and 1 × 8s, all No. 3 Common pine. Generally you also will find wider stock in the same grade stacked nearby. Using your tape measure, check the width and length of some of the boards.

This measuring process is very helpful during your initial visits to the lumberyard. It helps to familiarize yourself with the various widths and lengths of the available material. After a while, you will be able to identify width and even length by simply looking at a board. If you are like me, length is often something of a problem. I need to measure the length of a board when I buy lumber. On occasion, I can approximate length, but I always measure to be certain. Actually, this is probably a good practice in relation to the eventual cost of the board. Mistakes are made, especially in length of boards.

To continue with our lumber shopping example, find a stack of 1-×-6 No. 3 Common pine. Remember that the true dimensions of a 1-×-6 board are actually ¾ inch × 5 ½ inches. In selecting boards, you will need to pull off each board and look at both sides and the edges. It is important to remember that you are looking at No. 3 Common, so expect some flaws. Some of the visual flaws you will want in the board, but others you should avoid.

If the board is badly warped (Fig. 1-1), leave it. Sometimes you can see the warp as you look over the entire flat surface of the board. I often pick the board up and sight the length from one end to the other end. A very slight warp might be acceptable, especially if the board has other good qualities, for example, beautiful, tight knots. Make a judgment based on the project you will be making.

Other flaws you should look for are cracks or what sometimes amount to actual splits in the board (Fig. 1-2). You need to examine the entire length of the board, on both sides, for splits. Splits or cracks in the surface can, at times, be very difficult to see. Sometimes they will run only for a short distance in the board. At other times, they will penetrate the entire length of the board. What happens is that when you cut your 24-inch-long piece for the shelf top, you suddenly discover that you have two splintered 24-inch pieces. The board literally breaks into two pieces along the split.

Sap also can be a problem that you need to be aware of as you look over the boards. Boards that seem unusually heavy in relation to other boards of the same length and width frequently are loaded with sap. Leave them because they are useless for making projects. Finishes will not take or hold over sap. Also, you do not want a pocket of sap that will continue to drain or bleed on a finished project. These sap-laden boards often are tan to brown in color. Often they appear to be wet and even glossy in appearance. Many boards will have small pockets in them with sap bleeding out of them. If there are not too many of these pockets, portions of the board might be acceptable. There is no effective way to cover sap and keep it from seeping, however. It is best to leave these boards on the stack.

Knots are another major consideration in your selection process. Check knots to be certain that they are tight. Knots that have a black circle around their outer edges are often the kind that will fall out or pop out as you work on the board. A few knots that are loose or even a few knotholes in a board might be acceptable. Look at the board in terms of how much material remains usable. The kind of knots that you want in the board are generally reddish in color and are very tight. They appear to be an integral part of the wood. Size is not necessarily a factor, although sometimes the centers of larger, tight knots tend to partially break out. If they break out while you are working on the board, you can patch them easily with wood putty. Many of the larger knots are highly desirable for crafting, and simply require a bit more sanding during the finishing process. With a few exceptions, most good knots can be sawed through when necessary. It is preferable, however, to lay out your project in such a way that you avoid cutting through the knots.

One final word on the matter of knots. If you plan to do tole painting on your finished projects, you would be wise to avoid knots altogether. They tend to distract from the painted design and, often, are difficult to paint on. Most tole painters prefer perfectly clear boards.

Quite frequently as you examine pine boards, you will notice a narrow, rather long, reddish brown streak in the surface. Poke it with your fingernail; it very well might be rot. Sometimes the rot is sufficiently hard and will add to the overall attractiveness of the board. When it is soft or chips out, however, you might want to leave the board unless it is a rather small amount of surface. You frequently will work around some small areas of rot when you are laying out the project on the board.

For a host of reasons, boards sometimes will have a twist in them (Fig.

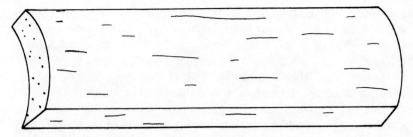

Fig. 1-1. Warped board.

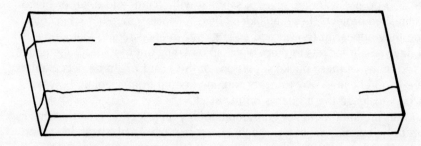

Fig. 1-2. Cracks and splits in a board.

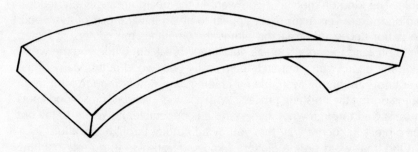

Fig. 1-3. A twist in a board.

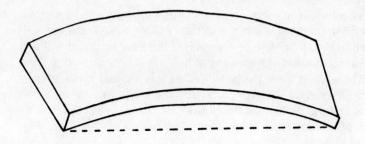

Fig. 1-4. A bow in a board.

1-3). Others, if you examine them carefully, will be bowed (Fig. 1-4). A slight twist or minor bow might be acceptable if the board has other redeeming qualities. On the other hand, if the problem seems severe, I would leave the board. These types of flaws often are caused by faulty drying of the lumber. They can present a real hazard when they are being cut on a radial arm or table saw.

Frequently you will notice that a portion of a pine board will have a grey color to it. It almost looks as if it were stained or painted grey. Normally, the grey color is from minerals taken in with the water through the root system of the tree. I think this greying enhances the beauty of a board, but it can present problems if you plan to stain your project. If you use a dark stain, the grey portions of the board will become almost black. A light stain or a natural finish is generally not affected by the greying. Whether you take a board with mineral staining in it is a matter of personal taste. Incidentally, tole painters tend to avoid boards having mineral stains.

Another thing you should always do as you examine boards is to check the actual width and thickness of the boards. Sometimes a board will be overplaned and be too thin. On occasion, the width also might be wrong as a result of the milling process. When in doubt, measure.

A final reminder from my own experience. You probably will need to haul your lumber in a car, so do not buy anything you cannot haul. Hauling lumber can be very dangerous and must be planned for ahead of time. I sometimes will cut a long board into two pieces I can use on the project I plan to make. Either carry a hand saw in the car or ask the lumberyard to cut the board for you. If material will extend behind the car, find a red flag and tie it on the board. Think safety.

Chapter 2

Tools and Crafting Supplies

Although many of the projects presented in this volume have been designed to be made with a few hand and small power tools, some can be crafted more easily with large, floor-model power tools. Obviously, the larger floor-model tools will greatly simplify the making of all the projects. In my own crafting, I use an assortment of small power tools, hand tools, and some larger floor-model power tools. This is not to suggest that you must have an array of power tools to undertake the various projects presented in this book. Rather, it is intended to suggest the range and diversity of tools that can be used in making small projects from pine. Most of the tools required are usually found in most households. Those that are not can be purchased with a minimal investment.

In addition to a diversity of tools, the various projects in this book lend themselves to varying levels of skill. Most of the projects are within the reach of the beginning woodworker who has limited or no experience with tools. If you will be making projects for the first time, it would be wise to use small power and hand tools initially. This approach not only minimizes your investment, it also eliminates the need to familiarize yourself with the more dangerous, complex, and expensive floor-model power tools. As you will discover in the brief overview of tools, there are numerous methods and tools the beginner can use. Although the woodworking process might be slower when hand and small power tools are used, it is just as effective and, in many ways, more fun.

It is a good practice to shop around at the various hardware stores in your community. This process not only helps you to understand what kinds of tools are available, it also gives you some sense of their prices. Very often the store employees are willing to provide additional information about the various tools they stock. It is also worth noting the range of tool accessories available in your local stores, since all woodworking tools usually require some type of accessory, ranging from a bit to a blade.

Mail-order catalogs provided by woodworking suppliers also are helpful in learning about tools and their various accessories. In addition to detailed descriptions of the various tools, they often provide information on how the tool can be used and what accessories are best. Catalogs also give you a good idea of the prices of the various tools and their accessories. A listing of some mail-order suppliers is provided in the Appendix.

If you already have a variety of tools and accessories, the projects in this book should be equally challenging. The various projects will afford you the opportunity to develop additional skills with your tools but, more importantly, allow you to make some very different projects. You might want to produce any number of the projects in quantity to sell at local shows. All of the project designs have been sold successfully at a wide range of craft shows, in addition to gift shops. It is an excellent way to support your woodworking hobby or to make some extra money.

Because the process of woodworking is a series of related functions, it seems appropriate to briefly discuss tools in this framework. Although various accessories can enable a tool to have a number of functions, most tools have but one function. It is these primary woodworking functions as well as the tools that will accomplish them, that are our concern. Although the listing of tools is by no means complete, it is sufficient to enable you to make the various projects presented in Chapter 3. Also note that there are additional functions to the woodworking process not mentioned here. Those that are described result in a process that will facilitate the making of small pine projects.

THE SAFETY FUNCTION

The safety function must overshadow all subsequent functions and the total woodworking process. The matter of safety cannot be overstressed. Never use any tool, whether hand or power, until you have a complete understanding of how the tool works and what hazards it presents to you. Carefully study the owner's manual that accompanies each tool, especially power tools. In the woodworking process, you are working with tools that are driving extremely sharp pieces of steel at high speeds. The potential for serious injury is always present. It is a good practice to develop a listing of medical specialists you can use in the event of injury. I have a listing of specialists that is prominently displayed by the telephone in case a shop accident should occur. Although I have never had reason to call on these specialists, I know how to reach them in the event of an accident. The displayed listing of names and their specialties also has a certain chilling effect that continually reminds me of safety.

Whenever you are using tools, you should use protective devices. Always wear a face mask or safety glasses when you are working with tools. Ear plugs or other devices to protect the ears from the high-pitched noises of power tools should be mandatory in your shop. Most of these safety devices are readily available at local hardware or discount stores. Purchase them before you start any woodworking activities. Incidentally, I often wear leather gloves when I am working with small, sharp hand tools.

Also in my shop, I have bright red signs with the word *Danger* on them placed over every power tool. Also, various signs that employ some vulgarity remind me of safety. You will find that these kinds of practices tend to keep issues of safety paramount in your shop. I also have several commercial fire extinguishers in the shop.

Although it is not my intention to terrify you before you even begin making your projects, it is my hope that you will deal realistically with matters of safety. Shop injuries are generally the result of carelessness with tools. Think and practice safety. It makes woodworking a lot more fun and certainly less painful.

THE MEASURING FUNCTION

Although measuring is one of the least dramatic functions in woodworking, it is clearly one of the most critical. Since measuring procedures are so obvious and attainable, it is easy to take them for granted. As a result, it is easy to become careless and make basic errors. Most problems in making anything from wood are the result of careless measuring. Incidentally, as you plan for the measuring function, do not rule out the use of the metric system. It is effective and very simple to use.

As I suggested in the discussion on selecting pine, a tape measure is almost mandatory. You need the capability to measure the length of boards when you are selecting them, as well as when you are laying them out to cut. A wide range of compact tapes is available that will permit you to measure lengths up to 25 feet or more. They are large enough to use in a lumberyard, but compact enough to use in a shop. Be certain the tape has at least 1/16-inch graduations marked on its surface. Although you might not need these smaller fractions often, they are worth having should an occasion for their use arise.

You also should have a couple of standard rulers with clean, sharp edges. I have found a 36-foot aluminum ruler to be useful in laying out projects. A 12-inch metal ruler with a rubber backing is also worth having around. On smaller projects, I tend to rely exclusively on the smaller 12-inch ruler. If it has a rubber backing, this type of ruler can be used for cutting glass and other tasks related to the projects. You should purchase a metal ruler, rather than

Fig. 2-1. Torpedo
level (courtesy of
Stanley Tools).

a wood one. Metal rulers hold their sharp edges, are graduated more accurately, and are less prone to breaking.

A try square is also useful in making the projects. Although you can make a try square easily, you might prefer to buy one. Another excellent device is a combination square. You need something that can correctly make a straight, vertical line from the edge of boards. This function becomes critical if you are sawing your boards with a hand or small electric saber saw. You need to have a good, straight line to follow when cutting. Combination squares enable you to make straight lines. They have other functions but, for the projects in this book, their use is limited to layout work. If you prefer a larger square for use in home remodeling as well as for the projects, you might want to consider purchasing a steel square.

There is an assortment of other clever and very useful devices for measuring that you might want to consider. For example, a school compass is an effective and inexpensive device for measuring circles for projects. When it is time to hang a shelf, you might want to purchase a small torpedo level (Fig. 2-1). These small levels, along with their larger counterparts, can be extremely useful in the woodworking process. There are all types of measuring devices that you can use for a variety of functions around the house. You will find them very helpful both in the shop and for hanging the various projects you make.

THE SAWING FUNCTION

The sawing function can be effectively accomplished with an array of tools. Although speed and accuracy are involved in sawing, the basic issue is whether you want to do it with a hand or a power tool. Since pine cuts considerably easier than the hardwoods, the use of hand tools is a very real option. You might be limited when you are cutting some of the detailed scrollwork on a few designs, but you can make most projects using various handsaws.

Handsaws

There are any number of handsaws available that can do your sawing of straight cuts, curves, and even some details. Many handsaws also can make cuts other than what they were designed to do. For example, a metal-cutting hacksaw can be used to make a straight cut in pine. The hacksaw is an excellent all-around tool to have available for a range of household projects. Other general-purpose saws that are relatively inexpensive are utility saws. These types of saws generally have a number of blades and can be used for straight cuts as well as curves. They also are effective for cutting internal holes in a project. As a rule, if a particular type of handsaw can do the job at hand, without danger to you, you can use it. Do not abuse the tool, but use it to accomplish the necessary task.

Better quality and more effective handsaws are available for either crosscut sawing or ripsawing. Each type of cut requires a different type of handsaw, for example a crosscut saw or a standard ripsaw. Many households seem to have one or both of these types of saws around. They are extremely effective for working with pine and are great fun to use.

Other handsaws that you might want to consider are the miter saw for straight cuts and the coping saw for curves. The miter saw, especially when used with a handmade miter box, is effective for both straight and mitered cuts. Of course, you might have a standard professional miter box (Fig. 2-2). Although miter saws are restricted in terms of the width they can cut, they can perform many sawing functions for a range of projects. The small coping saw, although initially difficult to use, can be extremely effective for cutting curves, especially in pine. Both the coping saw and replacement blades are inexpensive. As with any tool, you will find some practice is necessary for you to become an effective user of the coping saw.

A relatively new type of saw, at least to this country, is the Japanese

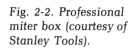

Fig. 2-2. Professional miter box (courtesy of Stanley Tools).

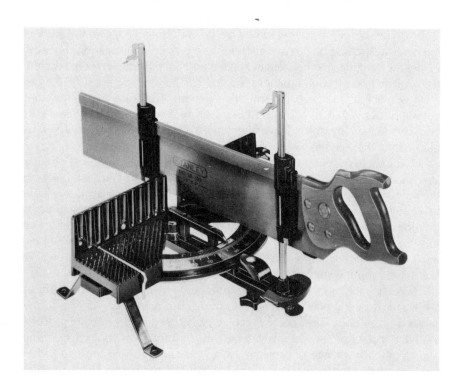

handsaw. This saw is available in a range of styles to make different cuts. Although somewhat expensive, it is extremely effective for a handsaw. A number of mail-order suppliers listed in the Appendix stock Japanese saws, in addition to the more traditional ones discussed earlier.

Power Saws

A preferable way to perform the various sawing functions for the projects in this book is to use a saber saw. A wide variety of these excellent and highly versatile small power tools are on the market. Basically, the saber saw is a hand-held power jigsaw that offers immense versatility to the crafter. Depending upon the type of blade used, you can make straight cuts, circles, angles, or any combination of cuts with relative ease. Although safety should be a primary consideration in the use of any tool, the saber saw is much less dangerous than many other kinds of power saws.

If you do not have a saber saw, you can purchase an adequate tool at your local hardware store or through a mail-order supplier. Frequently, through comparative shopping, you can purchase a much better tool for less money from a mail-order supplier. You will find that commercial-grade tools can be purchased often for little more than the standard hobbyist's tool. You might want to buy one that comes with an edge guide for making straight cuts. This device greatly increases the capabilities of the tool.

A major factor in the use of the saber saw is the type of blade that is used. You will be somewhat overwhelmed by the variety of blades on the market. I generally purchase blades designed for fine cuts or scroll sawing. Usually, blades are described by their length and the number of teeth per inch. I usually use a blade that is about 5 inches long and has 20 teeth per inch. The more teeth per inch a blade has, the smoother the cut. The reason I use the finer cutting blades is that, in addition to being more versatile in the types of cuts you can make, they also leave the wood edges relatively smooth, thus eliminating the need for a lot of extra sanding.

Two other types of power saws that can be useful are the hand circular saw and the electric miter saw. The hand circular saw is often found around the home of someone who has done remodeling. This type of saw is available in a range of blade diameters. It can be very effective for making straight cuts on pine of varying thicknesses. The power miter saw is an extremely effective tool for making either straight or miter cuts. It is a superb tool for making any kind of mitered frames. As with any power saw, use these tools only after you have carefully studied the safety procedures in the owner's manuals.

If you are inclined to the larger floor-model power saws, a radial arm or table saw is highly effective. These tools are not mandatory to any of the projects in this book. They do, however, greatly speed up the crafting process. With a circular saw, these tools can quickly perform all of your crosscutting and ripping for a range of projects. Also, you can use both tools for other types of sawing. In recent years, the radial arm saw has become very popular with the home owner and do-it-yourself woodworker. The standard table saw remains the tool of choice of the professional woodworker. If you are planning to make crafts to sell at local shows, you definitely should consider buying one of these larger saws. As an aside, the circular saw blade was invented by Sister Tabitha Babbitt, a Shaker, in about 1810. The circular saw blade represents one of the major contributions to woodworking.

Another floor-model tool that offers great versatility to the crafter is the band saw. In addition to crosscutting, this tool is ideal for ripping stock and resawing it. I frequently resaw standard ¾-inch-thick pine into ½-inch-thick material for use with projects. Generally, for resawing stock, you want to use a ½-inch-wide blade.

A related floor-model tool that can clean up the sawed surface or edges of a board is a jointer (Fig. 2-3). If you are developing a shop or considering making items for sale, you also might want to purchase a small planer. The planer will permit you to reduce the thickness of your boards very quickly and to exact dimensions. To minimize waste, after resawing a board on the band saw, I plane the cut surface. Although both jointers and planers are expensive, they are tools you might want to consider if you decide to get serious about woodworking. They are, however, not necessary to do the projects presented in this book.

The band saw also offers excellent capability for detailed scrollwork. You can make many decorative cuts using a ⅛-inch or ¼-inch-wide blade on a band saw. Using a self-made jig, I also cut large round pieces on the band saw. It is an ideal circle cutter when round pieces are needed for decorative or functional projects. Although the band saw is not mandatory for any of the projects in this book, it is one of the most useful tools in the shop. If you are planning to develop a shop someday, by all means include a band saw among your tools.

If you have one of the floor-model power jigsaws, you can make many of the projects in this book with relative ease. In recent years, a series of large jig or scroll saws using a range of new technologies have become available. The jig or large scroll saw is ideal for making decorative detail, but it is limited to this function. You still need another tool to make crosscuts and rips in boards. These larger tools are expensive but, again, are an excellent addition to any shop. If you are planning to make the projects in quantity, you might want to consider one of these larger floor-model scroll saws. They are available in a wide range of styles and prices.

Although this listing of tools is but a sampling, it should indicate that you can perform the sawing function with a diversity of tools. The way you accomplish the various sawing functions required by the projects will very much depend upon your ability and willingness to purchase tools. Fortunately, many households already have several of the tools just described. Your immediate problem might simply be learning how to use your tools effectively and safely.

Fig. 2-3. Jointer (courtesy of Delta International Machinery Corp.).

THE DRILLING FUNCTION

As with the sawing function, the process of drilling the various required holes can be accomplished with a variety of tools and accessories. In addition to the primary drilling tool, you can use a wide variety of bits for the projects. By way of accuracy, in woodworking, the drilling function is generally called *boring*. It seems, however, that most people tend to refer to making holes in anything as a process of drilling rather than boring.

Hand Tools

If you are inclined to use hand tools, the brace and bit are effective to achieve the drilling function. This hand-held tool is a delight for making holes. Although the user must provide the power, the brace and bit are extremely accurate and relatively easy to use. With this combination, you can generate large, interesting shavings that give you a real sense of working with wood. Unless you already have a brace and an assortment of bits, they can be rather costly. If you buy bits, be certain you purchase the kind required for a brace. Incidentally, never use a wood bit designed for a brace in a power drill. These bits are not designed or manufactured to function at the high speeds generated by electric drills.

 The brace, like many other tools, sometimes can be found at flea markets or auctions. If you find a used one, check to be certain that the chuck (the part that holds the bit) is all there and working. If it works, you might have solved your drilling problems with an effective and enjoyable tool. You will never get into mass production with a brace and bit, but you certainly will have a good time and make some fine projects.

 For making small holes for starting screws, a good device to use is a yankee drill (Fig. 2-4). This tool also is hand-powered, but is very effective for making small holes. Be sure to use only drill points specifically designed for the tool (Fig. 2-5). Another type of small hand drill, which can use standard high-speed steel bits, is also very effective (Fig. 2-6). You need a drilling capacity for making small holes for a number of projects. These types of tools are almost mandatory if you do not have an electric drill.

Fig. 2-4. Yankee drill (courtesy of Stanley Tools).

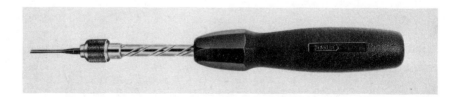

Hand Power Drills

The hand power drill is probably the one tool most people are likely to own. As with saber saws, the brands and types of power drills available are

Fig. 2-5. Drill points (courtesy of Stanley Tools).

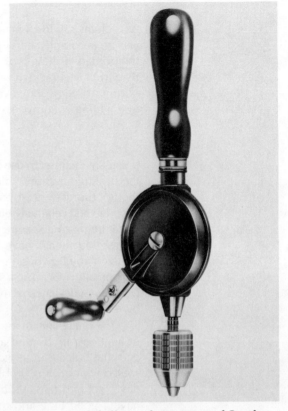

Fig. 2-6. Hand drill: crank (courtesy of Stanley Tools).

numerous. Many drills are designed, built, and priced for the homeowner/hobbyist market.

Be certain to check the various consumer reports and sources of shopper information if you find it necessary to buy a drill. Also check the catalogs of mail-order suppliers before you purchase a tool locally. Very often you can buy a commercial-grade tool for not much more than the hobbyist type. As a rule, the commercial tools have superior electrical components and bearings. They are generally built and designed for continuous use, whereas hobbyist tools can be overused easily. You will be more than satisfied with both the quality and longevity of commercial tools.

Hand electric drills are generally referred to as ½-inch, ⅜-inch, or ¼-inch tools. These designations relate to a number of factors. Primarily, they refer to the size of the chuck that holds the bit. Although bits might be almost any diameter, the ends that are held in the chuck are usually ½ inch, ⅜ inch, or ¼ inch. You must buy your bits in relation to the diameter your drill chuck will accommodate. The actual speed of the drill or bit also varies according to these designations. For example, a ¼-inch drill usually has a speed ranging from 1,600 to 2,800 revolutions per minute. These smaller drills generally revolve faster and have less power than the larger ones. If you need to buy a drill, you would be wise to consider purchasing a ⅜-inch one. They are more powerful and also allow you to use a greater variety of bits.

Another feature of hand power drills is *variable speed*. This feature allows you to control the speed of the drill bit by varying the amount of finger pressure on the trigger. Normally, the drill rotates clockwise. In addition to the variable speed, some drills have a reversing capacity. By simply pushing a switch on the tool, the bit will rotate counterclockwise. This is a very useful feature for extracting stuck bits and for removing screws.

Although a hand power drill is adequate for making the various projects in this book, you might have or prefer a floor-model drill press. As you might guess, these larger tools are considerably more powerful and enable more accurate drilling to be done. They are also substantially more expensive. A drill press can be an indispensable tool once you have used one. If you already own a drill press, it will serve you well in making the various projects in this book. There is no need, however, to purchase one for making projects from pine. A hand power drill, properly used and with appropriate bits, can accomplish the drilling tasks for all the projects. One distinct advantage of the drill press is that you can use a wide variety of accessories that the smaller tools cannot handle or accommodate.

One final type of hand power drill needs to be mentioned: the air-drive or pneumatic drill. In recent years, a variety of reasonably priced air tools have become available. They generally outlast and outperform electric tools. The only significant drawback with pneumatic tools is that you also need an air compressor. However, small 1-horsepower air compressors are becoming increasingly popular with homeowners. They provide sufficient air pressure for automotive uses, painting, and of course, pneumatic tools. I find my air compressor to be indispensable for blowing dust off pieces prior to finishing. They are also very effective for blowing dust from clothing. You might want to examine some of the available pneumatic tools if you already have an air compressor.

Bits

Major factors in the drilling function are the actual drills or bits that are required by the various tools. Again, there is an almost overwhelming variety of drills, bits, and drilling accessories on the market. For making the various projects in this book, you need only a few basic bits. Although the diameter required might vary among projects, the type of bits necessary are essentially the same.

Before you buy bits, examine the various mail-order catalogs that are available. Many companies sell commercial bits that are considerably less expensive than bits available at a local store. They also have a greater selection of quality wood bits.

Bits used primarily for metalworking are helpful in a number of the projects in this book (Fig. 2-7). Normally these bits are called *high-speed steel bits* and are available in a range of diameters and lengths. Extra-long bits, often called *aircraft bits,* are also readily available. I frequently use this type of bit to drill holes of ¼ inch diameter and less. A ⅜- or ¼-inch-diameter bit is excellent for drilling holes to receive a saber saw blade when you are making an internal cut in a project. As you will discover in the projects, the larger high-speed bits also can be very useful.

One problem with high-speed steel bits is that they tend to *skate,* or run around on the surface of a board. Their points are dull because they are not designed for immediate penetration. Because they are designed for use in metal, their points are rounded. You can eliminate this surface skating by making a slight indentation in the wood surface where you will drill the hole. When you need to use this type of bit with a project design, I will indicate specific sizes.

Spade bits, unlike high-speed bits, are designed for use in wood (Fig. 2-8). They are, however, available only in limited diameters. Although spade bits are by no means the most effective wood bore, you might want to use them because of price and availability. You frequently can find spade bits in local discount stores. One problem with spade bits is that they tend to slap the wood as you drill into a board. You will discover that, if you are not careful while drilling, the hole diameter will be a little larger than planned. For some projects, this lack of tolerance is usually not a problem. On other projects, you definitely will need more accuracy when you are drilling holes. Another advantage of the spade bit is that it can be resharpened easily with a whetstone or file. To keep your costs down, you might want to purchase some of these bits.

An excellent, but somewhat more expensive bit is the power bore bit (Fig. 2-9). This type of bit has an extra long point for precise and immediate penetration into a board's surface. The bit is designed to drill holes rapidly and cleanly, especially in soft wood. Power bores and space bits both have a ¼-inch-diameter shank that can be held in either a hand drill or a drill press. The power bore is available in diameters from ⅜ to 1 inch. I have used these bits over the years in crafting pine and have found them very effective. They would be an excellent choice to accomplish the drilling functions on the various projects.

No doubt the best all-around wood bit is the brad-point bit (Fig. 2-10). Some users refer to this bit as a *spur bit.* The center of the bit has a small, sharp spear that quickly penetrates the board's surface and holds the bit in place. The bit has two sharp spurs that do the actual cutting in the wood. The bit is spiral, so it enters the wood easily and also ejects the wood shavings.

The brad point is designed to work equally well in hard or soft woods. As with the other wood bits, brad points generally are available with diameters ranging from ¼ to 1 inch. The bits often are sold in sets, but they can be

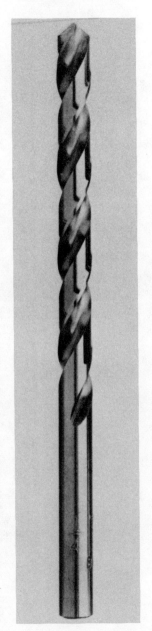

Fig. 2-7. High-speed steel bit (courtesy of Vermont American Tool Co.).

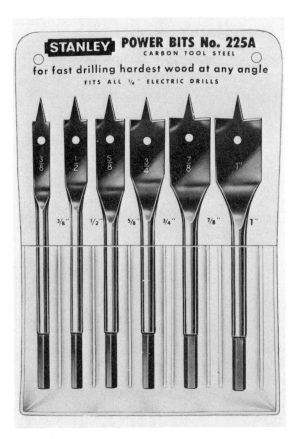

Fig. 2-8. Spade bits (courtesy of Stanley Tools).

Fig. 2-9. Power bore bit (courtesy of Stanley Tools).

purchased individually. Most brad-point bits are designed to fit a ¼-inch drill chuck. You might want to examine the various mail-order catalogs for these bits. They are generally available to most tool suppliers at rather competitive prices. If you need to buy bits for the projects in this book, I would recommend the brad points. Incidentally, you also can sharpen the brad points.

In recent years, another superb wood bit has become available in this country. The forstner bit has, until recently, been used primarily by European woodworkers (Fig. 2-11). These bits are designed to drill into wood at angles, into end grain, and even into knots. They are highly versatile and, unlike other wood bits, leave a flat-bottomed drill hole. The bit is extremely accurate, but can be somewhat difficult to align over a small mark on the board's surface. The center point of the forstner is very short. These bits are now available in diameters ranging from ¼ inch to 2 inches. If you can purchase quality forstners at a reasonable price, you might want to consider them for your drilling tasks.

A final bit to consider is the multispur machine bit (Fig. 2-12). Since these bits are generally manufactured with ½-inch-diameter shanks, they are usually

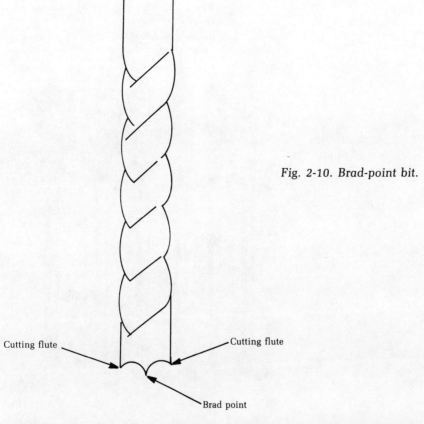

Fig. 2-10. Brad-point bit.

Cutting flute

Cutting flute

Brad point

limited to use on a drill press. They are, however, frequently used on a lathe. Multispur bits are fast cutting and can make a hole with a great deal of accuracy. You also can drill to a greater depth with the multispur than with other wood bits. Whenever you are using this type of bit, you must reduce the speed of the drill. You also should clamp the wood being drilled onto the drill press. Although expensive, multispur bits are long-lasting and can be sharpened easily. They are available in diameters of ½ inch to 2½ inches. Most mail-order tool suppliers carry a range of these bits. If you have a drill press, you might want to consider using these bits for your projects.

Drilling Accessories

In the context of the drilling function, a number of important drilling accessories also should be mentioned. One accessory that you might want to use is a plug cutter (Fig. 2-13). These small cutters can be used on both a hand drill or a floor drill press. Either way, be sure to clamp the wood. You

Fig. 2-11. Forstner bit (courtesy of Leichtung, Inc.).

26

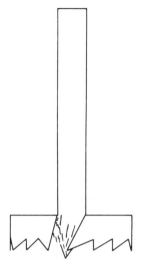

Fig. 2-12. Multispur bit.

Fig. 2-13. Plug cutter (courtesy of Stanley Tools).

can use plug cutters to make plugs of varying diameters to fill screw holes. You also can use them to cut plugs for decorative inlay work. You might prefer to buy commercial plugs, which are available from a number of suppliers, and eliminate the expense of buying a cutter. I have found the plug cutters to be an effective way of making my own plugs for projects. They allow you to cut plugs of the particular type of wood needed. Plug cutters are available in a range of diameters from ¼ to ⅝ inch.

Some type of countersink, to be used on either a hand drill or drill press, can be useful in making projects (Fig. 2-14). While countersinks are excellent for preparing screw holes, they also can be used to make hanging holes on shelf-support brackets. A more useful, but also more costly, way to countersink and drill at the same time is to purchase a drill and countersink set. I frequently use the countersink drill to make holes in exposed surfaces of accessories that are to be hung on a nail. It is a quick and efficient way to make a finished-looking nail hole through a project. Some of these and other uses of this device will become more apparent in the context of the projects.

Another useful device that is especially effective with pine is the hole saw. Hole saws are available in a range of diameters and can be used on either a hand drill or large drill press. For making small holes for a number of projects, a hole saw can be rather effective. When you are using this kind of device, you should always clamp the board being drilled. Frequently, the saw will grab an unclamped board and hurl it at the user.

A final drilling accessory that you might want to consider using with some projects is a circle cutter (Fig. 2-15). This device requires a drill press. Depending upon the size of circle cutter you purchase, you can cut circles to a diameter of about 8½ inches. It is imperative that you clamp the wood firmly to the drill press table when you use a circle cutter. The circle cutter is especially effective for use with pine. If you have a drill press, you might want to purchase a circle cutter for use with some of the projects.

Although there are numerous other devices available to assist you in making projects, the foregoing should provide you with an informed overview of some of the more useful ones. As you explore hardware stores and mail-order tool catalogs, you will discover there is an almost endless array of different accessories and bits to assist you in the drilling function.

THE ROUTING FUNCTION

Although this function is more appropriately called a *shaping* function, routing is more descriptive of how best to perform certain project tasks. The router is the tool of choice for accomplishing a range of shaping functions for most, if not all, of the projects in this book. This is not to rule out the use of a floor-model shaper. If you are planning to equip your shop for more sophisticated and production woodworking, a shaper is almost imperative. It is more likely, however, that a router is the tool most homeowners and hobbyists would own and have some experience using.

The router is the ideal tool for many necessary tasks in most of the pine projects. In fact, if so desired, you can use the router on all the larger projects.

If you are inclined to use hand tools exclusively, you might want to consider using either a block plane or a surfoam pocket plane. Both of these tools are very effective and affordable. Although they have only limited functions—for example, edge planing—they can be useful in making the projects.

In making the various projects, you will find a table-mounted router to be especially useful. When it is mounted under a table, a router can perform many functions that it cannot when hand held. If you have a router but not a table, you would be well advised to either make one or purchase one of the many commercial tables available. They are well worth having to increase the versatility of this multipurpose tool and to make the crafting of projects easier. You will find a router almost mandatory for much of the detail work on the pine projects.

Usually a router that is rated as 1 horsepower is more than adequate for making the various projects. Routers of this size generally have a ¼-inch collet to hold the various router bits. Most router bits are available with a ¼-inch-

Fig. 2-14. Countersink (courtesy of Stanley Tools).

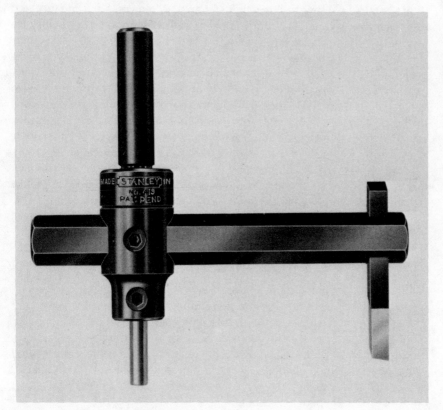

Fig. 2-15. Circle cutter (courtesy of Stanley Tools).

diameter shank that can be held in the ¼-inch collet. Although router bits are also available with ⅜- and ½-inch-diameter shanks, these larger bits generally are designed for more powerful routers. It would be to your advantage to shop the various mail-order supply catalogs if you need to buy a router or bits. A wide range of high-quality tools is available through mail-order suppliers.

In addition to a table for mounting your router, you will need a number of specific router bits for some of the projects. Router bits are available either in high-speed steel with carbide tip, or in solid carbide. Although carbide bits outlast the high-speed steel bits, they are also considerably more expensive. In selecting bits, you need to consider how often you will use them. If you will use them only occasionally, you might prefer the less expensive high-speed steel over the carbide. One advantage of high-speed steel is that it can be resharpened easily on a standard grinding stone. Carbide bits require special stones for sharpening. Although some of my bits are carbide, I usually buy the high-speed steel ones and sharpen them myself. For working with pine, the high-speed bits are more than adequate.

You will need to clean your bits more frequently when you are working with pine. The sap tends to collect rather quickly on the bit. Kerosene or a commercial solvent for cleaning bits is usually recommended for removing sap.

Although there are many different styles and sizes of router bits available, only a few different bits are necessary for making the pine projects. When a project requires the routing function, I indicate the type and approximate size of bit that works best for me. The following bits are some of the ones that I use most frequently.

The ⅜-inch or ½-inch round-over bit is used primarily for routing the edges of projects (Fig. 2-16). It probably is the most commonly used router bit for rounding over the edges of the various parts of a project. The ⅜-inch cove bit is an excellent alternative for routing edges on project components (Fig. 2-17). Although somewhat more decorative than a round-over bit, it gives edges a more formal appearance. The rabbeting bit, usually only available in a ⅜-inch diameter, is used primarily for mirror or picture frames (Fig. 2-18). It allows you to cut a rabbet or recessed area in a frame where either the mirror glass, picture, or frame glass is placed.

A ⅜-inch-diameter V-groove router bit is indispensable for making plate shelves (Fig. 2-19). The V-groove, along with a number of other types of bits, can be used to make a recess in the top surface of a plate shelf. The edge of the plates rest in the groove so they do not slide off the shelf surface.

For a more decorative edging on shelves and other projects, a roman ogee bit is very effective (Fig. 2-20). Some woodworkers tend to use the roman ogee almost exclusively on the edges of their projects. The chamfer bit also can be used to give an interesting effect to an edge (Fig. 2-21). It makes a clean, sharp taper on the edges of boards.

A multipurpose router bit is the ¼-inch straight bit (Fig. 2-22). The larger

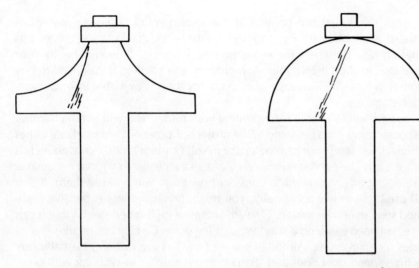

Fig. 2-16. Round-over router bit.

Fig. 2-17. Cove router bit.

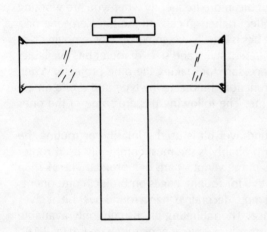

Fig. 2-18. Rabbeting router bit.

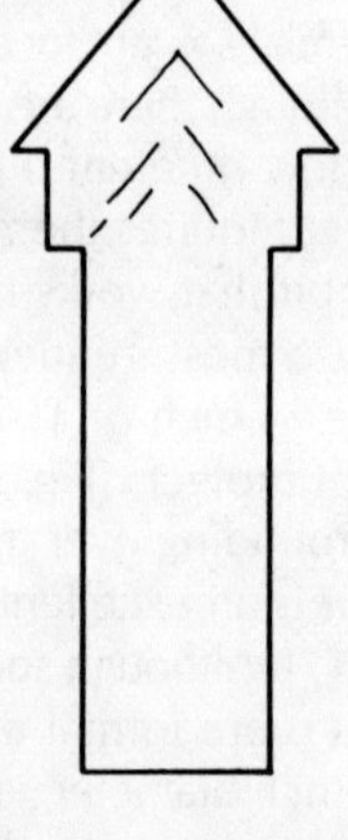

Fig. 2-19. V-groove router bit.

¾-inch-diameter straight or mortising bit is used less frequently than its smaller counterparts (Fig. 2-23). You will need one, however, for one very interesting project.

THE TURNING FUNCTION

The turning function is best accomplished with a wood lathe (Fig. 2-24). The lathe generally is used to make an entire project. Unlike many other large, floor-model tools, the lathe and the turning tools used with it confront the user with an exciting world of different projects. I will present some projects

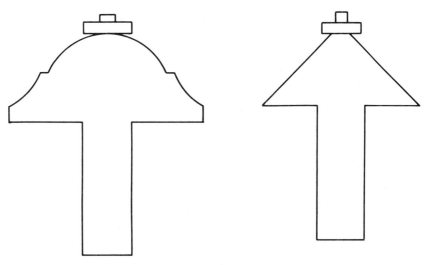

Fig. 2-20. Roman ogee router bit.

Fig. 2-21. Chamfer router bit.

Fig. 2-22. Straight router bit (¼″).

Fig. 2-23. Straight router bit (¾″).

to be turned from pine. If you have never turned pine on your lathe, this is a good time to start. It is an excellent turning wood and can result in some very functional and decorative projects.

If you are looking for a single tool for getting involved in woodworking, give serious consideration to the lathe. Although an expensive tool, it is one of the most satisfying and enjoyable ways of working with wood. The projects presented will serve to introduce you to only a few of the many possibilities the lathe holds for turning wood.

THE CARVING/WHITTLING FUNCTION

Although carving and whittling are actually two different ways of working with wood, for our purposes they are combined. As with wood turning, this is an area that also is a totally self-contained function. I have included projects to introduce you to this extremely enjoyable, relaxing, and satisfying way of

Fig. 2-24. Wood lathe (courtesy of Delta International Machinery Corp.).

working with wood. While pine is not the best wood for carving some pieces, it is more adequate for many others. Pine is also a good wood to use to develop some basic carving and whittling skills. As you will quickly discover when you begin exploring the world of carving tools, their numbers are almost overwhelming. In addition to the presented projects, you might want to examine some of the references presented in the Bibliography.

In addition to carving tools, there is a range of whittling knives available for the beginner. You might want to explore the literature of whittling. A number of books in the Bibliography discuss this fascinating method of working with wood.

One device that I have found useful with some of my projects is a *scorp* (Fig.2-25). This tool is extremely helpful for roughing out the bill of a wooden spoon. It also can be used for making small pine bowls. You will find that there are a great many different tools that can assist you in the whittling and carving function.

As you will discover quickly, one of the requirements of carving and whittling is being able to sharpen your knives and tools. Although I will briefly touch on this process in the projects, you would be well advised to do some additional reading. It is critical that your tools be extremely sharp. A dull tool or knife will not remove wood, and is very dangerous. Accidents happen in carving and whittling when your tools and knives are dull.

In recent years, increasing numbers of carvers have been using small electric tools for removing and shaping wood. For example, I frequently use either a commercial grinder and flex shaft tool or a Dremel tool. The small Dremel tool, along with drum sanders and various cutters, is extremely effective for both removing wood and shaping a project. Although it lacks the romance and the satisfaction of using knives or tools, this tool is effective and very efficient. If you already have a small moto tool, you might want to consider buying a router attachment and some microrouter bits. With them, you can carve on the surfaces of projects.

I have found that carving and whittling are very much like wood turning. Once you get started, you don't want to quit. They are fascinating and thoroughly enjoyable ways of working wood and relaxing at the same time. I usually wear thick leather gloves when I carve or whittle. This procedure grows out of experience. I would recommend that you use some protective gear for your hands.

Fig. 2-25. Scorp.

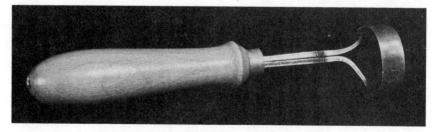

Although not a carving tool, one other device that is frequently used on carved pieces is a woodburning unit. Some carvers burn fine details into their carvings, particularly ducks. I frequently use a burning tool to enhance the lid of a box or the surface of some decorative project. You will be amazed at how many projects look a bit sharper or more attractive if you do some decorative woodburning on them. In a number of projects, I suggest the use of one of these devices. If you are interested in purchasing a woodburning tool, review the various mail-order tool catalogs. I use a rather inexpensive one that came with a child's project kit. It is not the best in terms of continuous heat or detailed work, but it does the job for me.

I hope you try some woodburning on one of your projects. I think you will thoroughly enjoy the process. By the way, do some practicing on scraps before you start on your finished project. Woodburning does take some getting used to, especially the first time you do it.

THE SANDING FUNCTION

Prior to assembling any of the parts of a project, you will need to sand the various surfaces. Abrasive papers and a number of tools to simplify this function are critical to a quality project. It is important to remember that you must remove the dust generated by sanding from all surfaces prior to gluing or applying any finishes.

Unlike many other functions in the woodworking process, sanding can easily be done by hand. You simply must remember to always sand *with* the grain of the wood. Most of the pine you buy for projects will need some sanding to clean and smooth the surfaces. Frequently there are stenciled grading marks on the board's surface. These marks are generally made with some type of ink and can be very difficult to remove. There are also any number of other marks and dirty spots on the surfaces that should be removed. Rough edges and sharp corners need to be lightly rolled with abrasive papers. Planing marks that give the board's surface a wavy appearance also need to be removed. You will find that finishing is much easier and the final project is more attractive when you properly sand a board.

Abrasive papers are available in a range of grits. The numbering system that is used for abrasive papers tells you how coarse or fine the abrasive grit is. Some manufacturers simply refer to their abrasive papers as being fine, medium, or coarse. As a rule, the coarser the grit, the lower the number given the paper. For pine projects, I often start with 80-grit abrasive paper, followed by 100 grit, and finally 150 grit. You might want to use 220 grit on some of the projects, depending upon how you will finish it. With pine, these grits are generally adequate. This does not mean, however, that the surface is ideal. You very well might want to use even finer grits on your projects. A major part of the sanding process is deciding how much time you want to spend doing it.

Most abrasive papers are sold in 9-×-11-inch sheets. This is the most economical way to buy abrasive papers. You can tear the piece into any number of smaller pieces for a particular job. Most general-purpose abrasive papers have aluminum oxide as the grit. This type of abrasive is excellent for use either by hand or with a power sander.

A block of wood with abrasive paper wrapped around it is an effective procedure for sanding flat surfaces. A piece of carpet pad is an excellent backing for abrasive papers when you need to sand rounded surfaces. Of course, commercial sanding blocks made from cork or rubber are available. I have found, however, that making your own sanding blocks is both easy and inexpensive.

If you prefer power sanding, you can find a variety of available hand and floor-model power sanding tools. A range of hand and floor sanders use abrasive belts of various sizes. If you have a belt sander, especially a large 6-×-48-inch floor model, you are well prepared to sand the projects. This type of large belt sander has become a rather popular tool of homeowners in recent years. If you are inclined toward production woodworking, you will find that the larger belt sander is almost mandatory. Most people, however, will have no need for such a large tool.

A palm or finishing sander is a type of power tool that you might want to consider purchasing. Small, electric finishing sanders are ideal for preparing the surfaces of projects. Most of them use a quarter sheet of standard 9-×-11-inch abrasive paper. In addition to local hardware and discount stores, shop the mail-order catalogs for these tools. There are usually some excellent buys available on either American or Japanese small power sanders. I always finish projects with these small palm sanders. They are effective, easy to use, and reasonably priced. It is hard to beat this combination in any tool.

Additional information and methods that are helpful in preparing projects for finishing are included in Chapter 4. You also might want to refer to some of the books in the Bibliography that deal with preparation of the surface for finishing. The final appearance of your project will be very much determined by how well you do the sanding function.

THE ASSEMBLING FUNCTION

While some projects require no assembly, others must be assembled using wood glue, nails, and sometimes screws. An array of products and devices is now available to help you assemble your projects with relative ease. You will find, however, that all projects do not need to be assembled in the same manner. How a piece is assembled is primarily determined by how the project will be used. With a large shelf, for example, you might want to use wood glue, nails, or screws. A small, decorative piece might require only glue for assembly. Items that will be subjected to constant use and stress need to be more securely assembled. Thus, as you approach the assembly of your projects, always review how you will use the piece.

Glues and Clamps

Glue is the primary product used in assembling projects. A range of high-quality glues is available, but the standard yellow-colored (aliphatic resin) wood glue is best. There are any number of companies manufacturing high-quality aliphatic resin wood glue. When you are purchasing glue, be certain it is wood glue and not general-purpose white glue. White glue is adequate for gluing mirrors into frames or securing paper as backing on mirror frames; however, you should always use wood glue for assembling projects. Most local discount or hardware stores stock both types of glue. Also, they are always available through mail-order tool suppliers. If you are planning to do a number of projects, buy the large containers of glue. Do not let the glues, especially the yellow wood glue, freeze because freezing will ruin it.

Although not mandatory, especially if you decide to use screws for assembling, clamps can be very useful. Whenever component parts of a project are glued together, they need to be clamped until the glue is dry. Clamping ensures a good bond between the pieces being assembled. A large variety of clamps are available to assist you in the clamping process. I have found the Jorgensen and Pony clamps to be very useful in my woodworking. The steel bar clamp is an excellent choice for general clamping work. Another excellent clamp for woodworking is the adjustable steel spindle handscrews. On larger projects, I usually use the adjustable Pony clamp fixtures that use black pipe. All of these clamps are available in a range of sizes, and they provide sufficient clamping versatility and holding power for pine projects. Clamps are not only effective for holding a joint together while the glue dries, they also allow you to clamp out a slight bow in a board when you are assembling.

Small C clamps also can be effective for clamping some of the smaller pine projects. These clamps are less expensive than bar clamps, but are also much smaller. You can, of course, buy them in a range of sizes. Before you buy any clamps, you might want to determine if you will need them for a particular project you want to make. Often screws and nails will eliminate the need for clamping.

Another device that can assist, not only in clamping but also in holding pieces that you are working on, is the wood vise. Although not a mandatory item for any of the projects, the wood vise can be extremely useful. To use it, you must secure it to a bench. You can use the vise to hold a piece of wood during the sawing process or while carving. Although various clamps can perform the same functions, a small wood vise can by very useful in the shop.

Nails and Screws

Although simple to use, nails can be rather complicated when it comes to knowing which type to use and when to use it. They can, however, be used with many of the projects in this book. Thus, some familiarity with them is important. Nails are highly standardized in terms of size, weight, length, type of head, and appropriate use. In addition to commonly used nails, you will discover that there are many specialty nails, such as screw nails or corrugated nails. For the projects, you need to be familiar primarily with finishing nails.

The size of nails is measured in a *penny* system, abbreviated *d*. This system was originally based on the number of a particular size nail that could be bought for a penny. Today, the smaller the number, the smaller the nail. For example, a 2d nail is 1 inch long, while a 60d nail is 6 inches long. Most hardware stores have charts depicting the various sizes and types of nails using the penny system.

The finishing nail is used primarily for indoor work, furniture making, and crafts. The head of the nail is not much wider than the body, and thus is easily driven under the board's surface. Driving the head under the surface is done using a nail set. Nail sets come with different diameters at their points for use on different sizes of nail heads. You can fill the nail hole with wood putty and thus remove any holes in the surface. In length, finishing nails are 3d (1¼ inches), 4d (1½ inches), 6d (2 inches), 8d (2½ inches), and 10d (3 inches). For most projects requiring finishing nails, 3d or 4d nails are usually adequate.

On occasion, you might want to use small brads and escutcheon pins. These and a range of other naillike devices are readily available and can serve important functions in the crafting process. A small tack hammer is useful for driving in finishing nails, wire brads, and small pins. It also helps prevent you from smashing your fingers with one of the larger hammers. You might want to examine the variety of these devices in your local hardware store. It is always helpful to have some idea of what is available.

For some projects, you might prefer to use wood screws instead of finishing nails. For example, you can easily assemble shelves using wood screws. When using screws, I drill a ⅜- or ½-inch-diameter hole in the board's surface to accommodate the head of the screw. After the screws are in place, I glue a wood plug of the appropriate diameter into the screw hole. I then sand the plug flush with the surface. This process hides the screws, and also gives the piece the appearance of a plug-assembled project.

Screws are highly standardized and available in a range of styles and different head configurations. Their primary advantage over nails is their holding power. They do, however, require considerably more time and effort to use than do nails. As a rule, I use flathead wood screws when a project requires this type of assembly. I also tend to purchase the least expensive screws. As a guide, a screw should penetrate the boards being secured by at least one-half of its length. Obviously, the more penetration, the better the holding power.

You might want to explore the range of available wood screws at a local hardware store. Flathead, Phillips wood screws are generally the easiest to drive into the wood. You also might want to examine some of the new square, recess screws. A good technique to ease the penetration of screws into wood is to rub a little soap on the threads. Be careful not to buy screws with a diameter that is too large for the thickness of the wood. It is very easy to crack a board when you are securing it with a screw that is too large.

If you are interested in using pneumatic tools and have an air compressor, you might want to consider a power nailer or stapler. Although these tools are for those who plan to make projects in quantity, they are excellent for assembling. I have used both a power nailer and stapler for many years. They greatly speed up the assembly process and secure the various parts with nails or staples coated with a substance to provide additional holding power. The nails and staples come in strips. Both are available in a range of lengths.

Although the foregoing discussion briefly presents the major functions and some of the tools used in the crafting process, it does not include the various issues and procedures for finishing the projects. Chapter 4 addresses the finishing function and also the various procedures and devices for hanging completed projects. More specific functions in the project-making process are discussed in detail in individual projects. Additionally, I will discuss a number of minor, yet critical, tools that are used with various projects.

CRAFTING SUPPLIES

Although you can craft most of the projects totally from lumber that you purchase at your local dealer, some projects require commercially made component parts. You might prefer to make some of these parts yourself. Following are commercial products, as well as suggestions to assist you in making these components.

In recent years, there has emerged a range of manufacturers and mail-order suppliers who specialize in crafting supplies. The range of these products, their quality, availability, and price make them ideal for use with your pine projects. Items or components that were previously available only to commercial wood-product manufacturers now are available to the general public. There are speciality items available for almost any project you might want to undertake. Any number of these items will be useful with the various projects presented in the next chapter.

One type of item that you will definitely want to consider purchasing is Shaker pegs (Fig. 2-26). These pegs are critical to a number of the pine projects that you will be crafting. The pegs, designed by the Early American Shaker community, are marvels of function and beauty. As you will discover in a number of the projects, Shaker pegs can be used for hanging bathrobes, cups, coats, or anything else that needs a place. Although you can make a similar functional peg from a standard dowel, the commercially available Shaker pegs make your crafting easier and, I believe, much more fun. The price of the commercial pegs makes them affordable for the hobbyist woodworker. You will find a number of mail-order suppliers of Shaker pegs

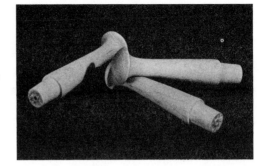

Fig. 2-26. Shaker pegs (courtesy of Woodworks).

Fig. 2-27. Candle cups
and brass rings (courtesy
of Woodworks).

Fig. 2-28. Gallery rails (courtesy of Woodworks).

and other components listed in the Appendix. Incidentally, Shaker pegs are also available in a range of sizes. When they are required for a particular project, I will indicate the necessary size.

Other wood component parts that you might want to consider buying are candle cups (Fig. 2-27). These and the brass rings that you can use with them are readily available from a number of mail-order suppliers. Although you can drill holes of an appropriate size to accommodate the base of a candle, these commercial cups greatly enhance your projects.

Gallery rail spindles, which can be used on plate shelves, are another delightful commercial item (Fig. 2-28). These small spindles are available in a range of sizes and greatly enhance a railing around the top surface of a shelf. Although you can use pieces of dowel, the commercial spindles present a more formal appearance to a finished shelf.

Screwhole plugs and buttons are other commercial items that you might want to consider. Although you can cut plugs with standard plug cutters on a drill press, the commercial ones are easier to use and more uniform in size. The small wood buttons provide an attractive touch to a number of projects.

There are many other commercially available components that you might want to use with your projects, but the ones listed here can be used with the presented projects. You will find, as you explore the various mail-order catalogs, that the variety of component parts available is a veritable bonanza for the home crafter.

For many years, I have ordered most of my crafting supplies and tools from mail-order suppliers. In general, the companies have been reliable and guarantee their products and service. An added feature of mail-order shopping is the availability of toll-free telephone numbers. Most companies are also willing to discuss their products via toll-free numbers. To facilitate your shopping, almost all accept national credit cards.

As you will find in the Appendix, most mail-order companies have catalogs and other descriptive literature of their products. Usually there is a charge for the catalog, but the amount is often deducted from the first order you place. Given the cost of printing and postage, it is not unreasonable for suppliers to charge for their catalogs. I also have found that catalogs from many of these companies can be an effective way to learn about woodworking. Another significant aspect of mail-order catalogs is the fantasy value they can provide. They represent the ultimate wish book for anyone who is faintly interested in woodworking.

The Appendix includes a sampling of mail-order supplies of both crafting products and tools. It also provides a listing of various woodworking magazines.

Chapter 3

Projects from Pine

Unlike other crafting books that provide very detailed plans and precise dimensions for wood projects, this book will approach the tasks somewhat differently. In part, small pine projects do not require this type of crafting detail. Also, projects that are Country in theme probably look better if they are somewhat rough dimensionally and in design. They certainly are much easier to make. For each project, a photograph of the assembled piece is presented to assist you. In some instances, the pictured project will be stained and finished. Other project pictures will present items that are unfinished. The various projects that are designed for the tole painter are unfinished and unpainted. Although I will make narrative suggestions regarding possible use of the projects, I do not include the specifics on painting. Throughout this chapter, when necessary or deemed helpful, I will present drawings of component parts or assemblies, with some dimensions. On occasion, there are also drawings of alternative designs.

I will suggest general materials and supplies necessary for making a particular project. I also will give a number of specific tasks that are deemed critical for a project, along with suggestions for tools and their usage. Additionally, I will provide few tips and an occasional shortcut. However, an overriding theme of my approach to making small pine projects is to encourage you to use your own resources and creativity. Much of the pleasure in woodworking is to solve the problems of your projects and have the opportunity to use your own imagination in designing and crafting your work.

My approach not only makes the entire process more satisfying, but also will be more practical: you can make things in the size and way that you want and need. You are encouraged to redesign them to dimensions that you want. You are making projects for your house, and your needs should determine the dimensional and design outcome of the project.

This approach to making projects will, in part, eliminate the constant worry of doing something wrong—of making a mistake. Failures are usually the result of trying to exactly duplicate something that another person has designed. Frequently, in trying to follow all the intricate details of a project, you become frustrated, fail to do things according to directions, and generally have a miserable time. I prefer that you concentrate on and enjoy the wood and the process of woodworking. Make your projects, using the general designs and dimensions as ideas, in the way that you want them to look. This approach in making projects greatly reduces the inappropriate fears of making a mistake and, frankly, makes for better final pieces.

As you will note, each project is numbered and has a brief descriptive heading. To eliminate duplication of some detailed procedures, I will state them once and provide a reference to them when required by a later project. For example, I will give the procedures for using a table-mounted router to round-over the edges of a board but once. Later projects that require the same procedure will have only a reference to the earlier discussion. You might want to refer back to it to brush up on the various procedures. Hopefully, after you have done the procedure once, you will not need to refer to earlier discussions.

One final note before you begin the actual crafting process involves the use of patterns. Patterns are rather fun to make, and they are critical to the designing and crafting process. They ensure uniformity of size and design, and they also make sawing the needed piece substantially easier. Heavy construction paper is excellent material for making initial patterns. This type of paper is sufficiently durable, but it is also easy to cut with a pair of scissors. Patterns using this type of paper allow you to explore ideas and possible designs with relative ease and without wasting wood. They enable you to get some perspective of size and appearance before you begin the actual crafting process.

Always make patterns to the actual desired size of the part or design and then trace the pattern onto the wood's surface for cutting. In the cutting function, you simply follow the traced pattern lines. The only other consideration in using patterns is to trace them with the grain of the wood, rather than across the grain.

PROJECT 1: ADJUSTABLE BOOK ENDS

Although the adjustable ends of these book ends are somewhat plain in design (Fig. 3-1), they do offer considerable surface for tole painting or other types of embellishment.

You might want to consider using this project to hold recipe books in the kitchen. On the other hand, a small book shelf can be useful in almost any room in the house. In addition to thinking about how and where the project would be best used, you can explore different end designs. The ends can be designed to accommodate a particular tole pattern. They can also be designed around some theme to reflect their room placement. Spend some time designing your project to reflect both need and possible location. Figure 3-2 presents the project along with some suggested dimensions.

[1] Use 1-×-6 stock for the end pieces.

[2] You need to make a pattern for the end pieces. Although you can draw one freehand directly onto the board, it is somewhat easier to make one using construction paper. Use the outline in Fig. 3-2 as a guide for your pattern. You might prefer to modify the design or even change its dimensions. The pattern should be at least 7 inches high in order to provide adequate support for the books.

[3] Measure and cut the end pieces to a length of 8 inches. This length will allow an extra 1 inch for purposes of patterning and cutting. Trace the end pattern on both boards and cut. A saber saw is effective for cutting the detail in the design.

Fig. 3-1. Adjustable Book Ends.

[4] Cut two pieces of ¾-inch-diameter dowel to a length of 12 inches. This length and diameter are the suggested project dimensions. Of course, you might prefer to use other dimensions based on your earlier planning activities.

[5] Carefully lay out the location of the two dowels that penetrate the ends. You must drill two ¾-inch-diameter holes through both end pieces. When the project is assembled,the dowels pass through these holes. Refer to Fig. 3-2 for the approximate location of the dowels. The dowels should be precisely placed, so measure and mark the location of the holes before drilling. In part, the placement of the dowels is determined by the size of books that will be placed in the holder.

[6] Use a ¾-inch-diameter wood bit to drill the holes. Be certain to place a support board under the end pieces while you are drilling the holes.

After you have drilled the holes, test the dowels in them for fit. If they are too tight, widen the holes using either abrasive paper or a round wood

Fig. 3-2. Side and end views of the Adjustable Book Ends.

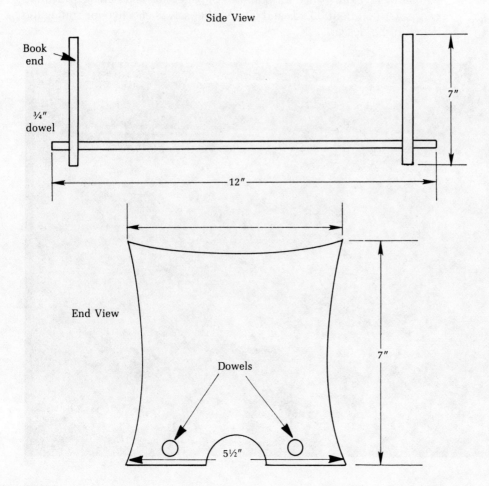

Side View

Book end

¾" dowel

7"

12"

End View

Dowels

7"

5½"

rasp. The dowels should move freely in the drilled holes so you can adjust the book ends as needed. Sand the end edges of the dowels round.

[7] Rout or sand the edges on both sides of the end pieces.

[8] Sand all the edges and surfaces to a finishing readiness.

PROJECT 2: CLIPBOARD

A clipboard (Fig. 3-3) is one of those projects that has a variety of uses. In addition to its use as a writing surface, it is an effective device to secure important notes or other papers for future reference. The board uses a strong spring clamp that will hold a sizable collection of papers or a large pad. The metal clip is available from a number of the mail-order suppliers listed in the Appendix.

The actual size of the board can be determined by specific need. The sample project is designed to hold standard 8½-×-11-inch paper. You might prefer to make it longer so it will accommodate a large pad. Figure 3-4 presents the project design along with dimensions.

Fig. 3-3. Clipboard.

[1] The project requires 1-×-10 stock. Recall that a 1-×-10-inch board is actually 9¼ inches wide. This width is adequate for holding 8½-inch-wide paper, along with most standard sizes of writing pads.

The board should be at least 14 inches long. In part, the length is determined by the type of clip you use. Some of the clips take up at least 2 inches

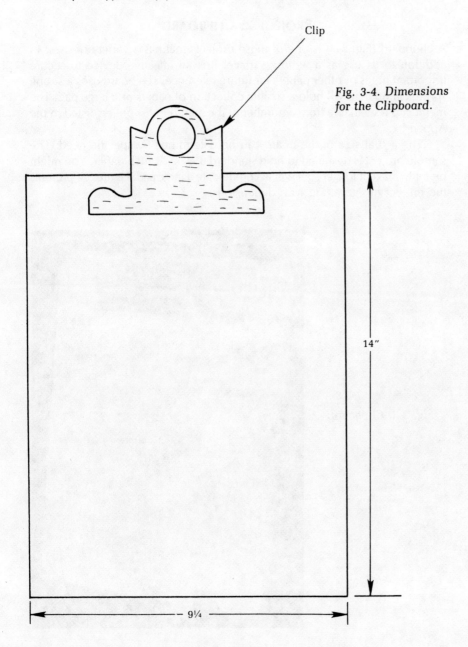

Clip

Fig. 3-4. Dimensions for the Clipboard.

14"

9¼

of the top surface of the board. Be certain to check the space needs of the clip before determining the final length of the board. Also, if a standard writing pad is to be used, you might want to increase the length by at least 1 inch. Plan the dimensions in relation to the clip and type of writing material you plan to use with the board. For our sample project, cut a piece of 1-×-10 stock to a length of 14 inches.

[2] Round the four corners of the board. Rounding not only enhances the appearance of the board, but also eliminates the dangers of having sharp corners. Cut all the corners the same.

An effective procedure for making the round corners is to make a curved cutting line on one corner. Using a saber saw, cut off the corner along the line. Then use the small piece that is cut off as a pattern for the other three corners. This procedure will ensure uniformity.

[3] Using a round-over bit and a table-mounted router, rout all the edges on both sides of the board. Do not remove too much of the edge while routing. Many people tend to over-rout the edges. Give them a slight roll, but don't remove too much wood.

[4] When routing is completed, sand the edges and the surfaces to finishing readiness.

[5] Center the clip on the front surface of the board. Measure and mark the center of the board near the top edge. Measure the length of the clip and mark its midpoint. Using wood screws with round heads, secure the clip to the board. Be certain the screws are not too long for the thickness of the board. You should not have to drill pilot holes for the screws; however, you might want to use a screw starter to make small indentations into the wood. Take your time with this procedure so that the clip is properly centered and secured adequately to the board.

PROJECT 3: SMALL HEART BOX

The Small Heart Box (Fig. 3-5) is only one of any number of small boxes that can be made from standard 2-×-4 pine. Although the heart is an obvious and clearly very popular shape for a small storage box, it represents only one of many possible designs. You might prefer to make a small square or rectangular box as an alternative to the heart. Other designs include animals, vegetables, fruit, or even birds. Think in terms of a basic shape that you can design in profile and make into a box. As you do some planning and design work, I think you will be amazed at some of the possible box shapes that will emerge. Use your imagination.

While the project box is small, it is sufficiently large to hold rings, earrings, or other small jewelry items. The box has a 1½-inch-diameter hole drilled in its center as a storage compartment. In addition to its storage capacity, the box presents sufficient surface for a small, but delicate, painted design. This should be an ideal small box for tole painting or woodburning.

Because the lid piece is sawed from the base of the box, a band saw is almost mandatory for this design. The lid is opened and closed by using a ¼-inch-diameter dowel system. The lid actually slides to the side of the box as it is being opened. More about this shortly. Figure 3-6 presents the profile of the box, along with its dimensions. If you prefer to make a larger box, consider using 2-×-6 material.

[1] Because the box is only 3 × 3 inches square, you will need but a small piece of 2-×-4 material. Very often you can obtain pieces of scrap 2-inch stock that is being discarded at construction sites. Possibly you have some pieces of 2-×-4 material lying around from a previous project. You also might want to consider making a number of boxes at the same time.

Measure and cut the box piece to a length of at least 3½ inches. This additional length makes it much easier to pattern and cut the box.

[2] So that the heart will be an attractive and balanced shape, it is necessary for you to make a pattern. An easy way to make a heart pattern is to fold a piece of construction paper in half. Mark the length of the box along the folded line. Measure one-half the width of the box from the folded line and make a mark. Draw half of a heart between these dimensional marks. Keeping the paper folded, cut out the traced half heart. Open the cut-out piece and you should have a perfect heart of the proper dimensions.

[3] Trace the heart on the 2-inch box material. You will need a band saw or a scroll saw to cut the heart pattern from the 2-×-4 material. If you are using a band saw, use a ⅛- or ¼-inch-wide blade. Cut out the heart.

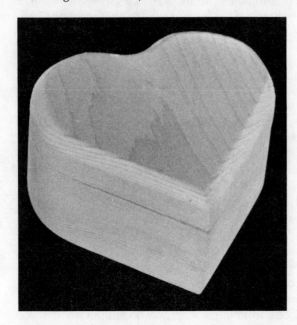

Fig. 3-5. Small Heart Box.

[4] Because the band-saw blade will mark the side of the box, you will need to sand the box. Usually the back portion of the heart needs the most attention. Go over the side with a range of abrasive grits and bring it to a finishing readiness. Be certain to remove all the saw markings.

[5] You will use a ¼-inch-diameter dowel for the hinge on the box; thus, you must drill a ¼-inch-diameter hole into the box and its eventual lid piece. Drill the hole in the upper portion on one side of the heart, entering the box from the bottom surface. Figure 3-7 presents a side view of the dowel system. In addition to the dowel hole, note the thickness of the lid and how the drilled

Fig. 3-6. Top and side views of the lid for the Small Heart Box.

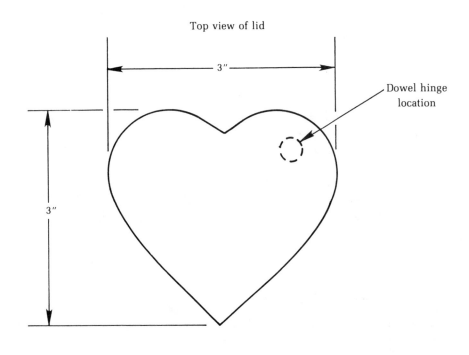

Top view of lid

— 3″ —

Dowel hinge location

3″

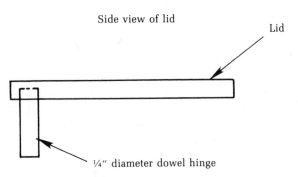

Side view of lid

Lid

¼″ diameter dowel hinge

hole penetrates it. Refer to Fig. 3-6 for the approximate location of the dowel in the upper portion of the box.

Using a ¼-inch-diameter brad point drill bit, drill the hole from the bottom surface to within ⅛ inch of the top surface. You will want to set the depth gauge on your drill press for this function.

If you accidentally drill through the lid, you can still use the box. The dowel end will simply be exposed on the top surface of the box.

[6] Next cut the lid piece to a thickness of at least ⅜ inch. This procedure is best done on the band saw with the fence in place. Set the fence to allow for a ⅜-inch cut. Remember to cut the lid from the top section of the box. The drilled hole entered the bottom section of the box. Carefully saw the lid piece from the box. You want a nice straight cut so take your time. Although you can make the cut with a ¼-inch-wide band-saw blade, this type of resaw activity is best done with a ½-inch-wide blade. Pine is sufficiently soft to permit some resawing with a ¼-inch blade.

[7] Sand both the bottom surface of the lid and the top surface of the box. You need to remove the saw blade marks. Do not, however, sand off too much wood. You want the lid piece to fit neatly on the top of the box. Also, don't round the edges where the two pieces come together.

[8] Cut a ¼-inch-diameter dowel to a length of ¾ inch. This piece will serve as the dowel hinge. Cut another piece that is approximately ¼ inch long. Glue the smaller piece into the hole in the bottom surface. It simply fills in the hole to give the bottom a more finished appearance. Sand the ends of the dowels slightly round so that they will fit more easily into the drilled holes.

Fig. 3-7. Side view of the Heart Box.

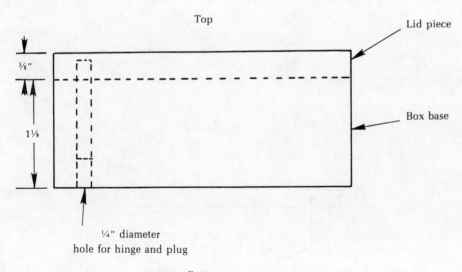

Top

Lid piece

⅜"

1⅛

Box base

¼" diameter
hole for hinge and plug

Bottom

[9] Using either a toothpick or wood splinter, spread wood glue in the lid dowel hole. Tap the ¾-inch-long dowel into the hole. Be certain the dowel is erect in the hole or there will be a gap between the lid and the box surface. Allow the glue to dry completely before testing the dowel for fit. If the glue is not dry, the dowel will twist from the hole.

[10] Place a touch of glue in the hole in the bottom of the box and tap the small dowel piece into the hole. After the glue is dry, sand the bottom to make the surface and the dowel end flush.

[11] Carefully twist the lid dowel into the box hole. If it is too tight, sand its entire length until it fits. If the dowel is too snug in the hole, it will twist from its glue bond in the lid. Take your time with this procedure until the lid opens easily. Don't force it.

[12] Drill a ½-inch-diameter storage hole in the center of the box. If you have a drill press, use a multispur or similar bit. If you are using an electric drill, a spade bit might be the accessory of choice. Leave a bottom thickness of at least ⅛-inch. Be careful that you don't drill all the way through the bottom of the box. Remember that most bits have a point that extends beyond the bit proper. Don't let the point penetrate through the bottom as you're drilling the storage hole.

PROJECT 4: SMALL BOX

This project (Fig. 3-8) is designed to assist you in making boxes of any desired size. Once you understand the various tasks, you can very easily increase or decrease the size of the design. Boxes are great fun to make.

In addition to being functional units for storing a range of items, the box lids present an excellent surface for tole painting, carving, or woodburning. You might want to design a box to suit a particular pattern you have in mind. Box lids truly can be showcases for a range of decorative embellishments.

The Small Box also provides you with the opportunity to use either miter or box joints. If you prefer mitered joints, you will need a miter box and saw or a jig that can be used on a table or radial arm saw. The ideal mitering tool is the electric miter saw (Chapter 2). To keep the project simple, the sample box will employ traditional butt joints.

The box walls are made from ¼-inch-thick batting. This is an excellent material for making boxes of any size. The batting used for this project is 1⅜ inches wide. The box lid is made from a piece of 1-×-4 stock. The lid is rabbeted using a table-mounted router and a ¼-inch rabbeting bit. This procedure results in a tenon that neatly fits inside the box when the lid is in place. The bottom piece of the box is also made from 1-×-4 stock. Figure 3-9 presents the box and lid, along with dimensions.

[1] For the box sides, cut two pieces of 1⅜-inch-wide batting to a length of 4 inches. Also, cut the two end pieces to a length of 2 ½ inches. Remember

to use batting that is ¼ inch thick. If you have a band saw, you can cut your own material to a ¼-inch thickness. It is best to use a 1-inch-wide blade for this type of resawing.

[2] Using wood glue, assemble the walls using the butt joints shown in Fig. 3-9. Spread glue on the ends of the end pieces and the inside surfaces of the side pieces. Assemble the pieces together.

[3] To hold the assembly while the glue is drying, use two large rubber bands. Simply stretch the bands around the assembly. Place one near the top edge and the other near the bottom edge. Rubber bands make excellent clamps for small items, especially boxes. Leave the bands in place until the glue is dry. Wipe off any glue that squeezes from the joints.

[4] Measure and cut the lid piece and the bottom section of the box. Use 1-×-4 stock for these parts. To be certain your pieces are exact, measure the top or bottom of the box frame. Remember to measure the outside of the frame. Use these dimensions for preparing the lid and bottom pieces. This procedure is an effective way to maintain accuracy in making the box.

[5] Spread glue on the box edges for attaching the bottom piece. Place a small bead of wood glue on the inside surface of the bottom where the box frame will make contact. Join the assembly together and clamp using large

Fig. 3-8. Small Box.

rubber bands. Wipe off any glue that squeezes out of the assembly. Allow the glue to dry.

[6] To make the tenon on the lid, you will need a rabbeting bit that will make a ¼-inch-long cut. As you might recall, this length is also the width of the box walls. It is best to use a table-mounted router for this procedure. Rout the top piece on all four sides in order to make the tenon. The routed tenon will fit neatly inside the box frame. The tenon only needs to be ⅛ inch long; however, you may make it a bit longer if desired. Usually an ⅛-inch tenon is long enough to hold the lid in place. Incidentally, you should not make too deep a cut with a rabbeting bit. It is best and safer to make several light cuts instead of one deep cut. Take your time with the routing function.

[7] After the tenon has been made on the lid, test it for fit in the box frame. If it is too tight, lightly sand the tenon walls until you have a good fit. Don't remove wood from the box walls. It can ruin the appearance of the box.

Fig. 3-9. Design of the Small Box.

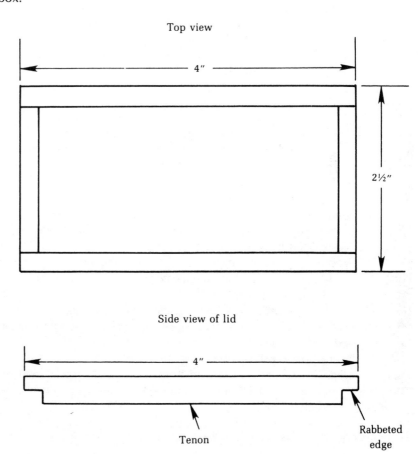

Top view

4"

2½"

Side view of lid

4"

Tenon

Rabbeted edge

[8] Using a round-over bit, rout the top edges of the top piece and the edges of the bottom section. Don't rout too much wood away. Simply make the edges slightly rounded.

[9] Using a range of abrasive grits, sand all the surfaces to a finishing readiness. Be certain the bottom piece and the lid are flush with the box walls. If not, sand them flush.

PROJECT 5: MAGAZINE HOLDER

The Magazine Holder (Fig. 3-10) is both very functional and decorative. It is sufficiently large to hold a quantity of magazines in a range of sizes. You might want to build the project to the suggested dimensions rather than redesign it. Its size is more than adequate for most households.

While I make large holes in both end pieces of the holder, you might prefer to cut a heart or some other design into them. These types of decorative touches greatly enhance the overall appearance of a project of this size. The holes also make it easier to pick up the holder when it's full of magazines. Give some thought to how you want the end pieces to appear.

You can make the strips on the sides of the holder from either standard ¾-inch-thick stock or from ⅜-inch-thick material, depending on whether you have a band saw to rip the stock. Either way, the holder looks very good. Figure 3-11 presents the holder and its dimensions.

[1] Make the ends and bottom pieces of the holder from 1-×-6 stock. Measure and cut the two ends to a length of 12 inches. Next, measure and cut the bottom piece to a length of 11½ inches. Angled cuts are not necessary even though the holder appears to use them.

[2] Make a pattern for the scrolled sides on the end pieces. If you prefer, measure and lay out the curved areas on one of the end pieces and cut. Use this finished end to pattern the other end piece. This procedure is sometimes easier than making a pattern.

[3] If you prefer the holes in the end pieces, make them with a circle cutter using a drill press, or cut them out using a saber saw. If you use a saw, pattern the holes and drill a pilot hole through the pattern to receive the saw blade. Cut along the patterned line. As suggested, you might prefer to prepare and cut a heart design in the end pieces. Whatever design you decide to use, be certain the holes are centered on the ends.

[4] Cut the six side strips (three on each side) to the various lengths indicated in Fig. 3-11. It is best to cut them at least ½ inch longer than required. The strips should be at least 1½ inches wide. You might want to use either 1-×-4 or 1-×-6 material for the strips. Cut them to width using either a band saw or a saber saw using its guide.

[5] Rout all the edges of the end pieces using a round-over bit. You should also rout the decorative holes in the end pieces. The bottom section

does not need to be routed. The outer edges of the side strips need to be routed also. Take your time with the strips if you are using ⅜-inch-thick material.

[6] Sand all the surfaces and edges to a finishing readiness. You might want to use a small electric pad sander for this procedure. This project has considerable surface to sand. Use a range of abrasive grits.

[7] Although it is somewhat awkward, glue and nail the end pieces to the ends of the bottom section. Use finishing nails for this procedure. Remember that the ends need to be at an angle to the bottom piece. This will result in a slight gap between the bottom section's ends and the end pieces.

[8] Before the glue is dry, secure the top side strip to the sides of the end pieces. Place it just below the bottom edge of the cutout areas on the ends. The strip should extend approximately 1 inch beyond the outer surfaces of the end pieces.

The next strip is the shortest one and it covers the side of the bottom piece. Glue and nail it in place. Remember to place it so it extends equally beyond the end pieces on both sides. Refer to Fig. 3-11 for the placement of this strip.

Fig. 3-10. Magazine Holder.

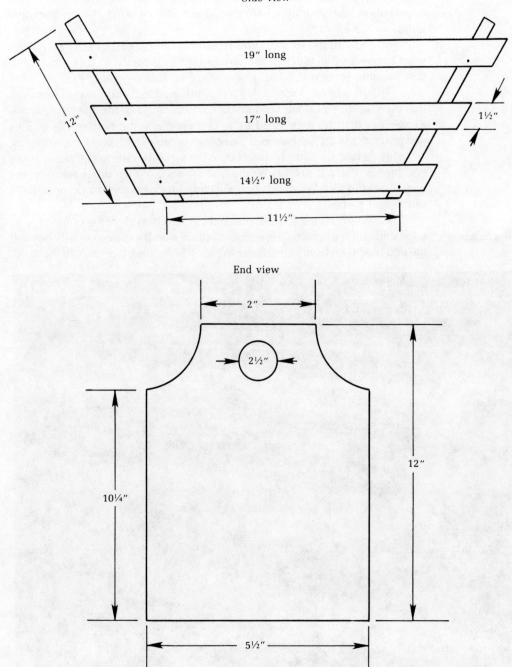

Fig. 3-11. Side and end views of the Magazine Holder.

Center the middle strip between the other two and glue and nail it in place. Repeat this entire process on the other side of the holder. Be certain to wipe off any excess glue that squeezes out from the strips.

[9] Using a saber saw, cut off the ends of all the strips at an angle that is equivalent to the end pieces. Each strip should extend the same distance from the outer surfaces of the holder's ends.

[10] Sand the cut edges of the strips slightly round. Also sand the inside edges of the strips since they will be somewhat splintered from the sawing function. There might be other areas on the holder that need a bit more sanding as well.

PROJECT 6: HANGING TELEPHONE BOOK HOLDER

The Hanging Telephone Book Holder (Fig. 3-12) is a functional piece that can be hung on the end of a counter or on the wall near the telephone. It is designed to accommodate telephone books of an average size. The very large, metropolitan-type directory will not fit in this design. Given its size, I'm not certain you would want a hanging holder to accommodate it. Prior to beginning the project, you might want to check the suggested dimensions against your local telephone directory. Some modification of dimensions might be necessary.

If you prefer a hanging magazine holder, this project can also function in this capacity. The dimensions will accommodate several large magazines or any other publications you might want to place in the holder. As already suggested, you might want to change the project dimensions to meet some special need. Do some planning for the project, both in terms of the size holder needed and the place where it will be hung. You might need to reduce the dimensions in order for the holder to fit in a particular location.

The project is made from standard stock that is ¾ inch thick. If you have the tool capacity, you might want to resaw material to a thickness of ⅜ inch. You can use this thinner material for both the front and back strips. Using material of this thickness reduces both the size and weight of the holder. Figure 3-13 presents the project, as well as its dimensions.

[1] The project is best made from 1-×-6 boards. This size stock will help minimize sawing and material waste. Measure and cut a piece to a length of 12 inches. Using either a band saw or a saber saw with a guide, rip this 12-inch board into two equal pieces that are approximately 2 ¾ inches wide. (Recall that a 1-×-6 board is 5½ inches wide.) These two 12-inch pieces are the sides of the holder.

[2] Measure and cut another piece of 1-×-6 material to a length of 10 inches. Saw the piece in half so that you have two pieces that are 10 inches long and 2¾ inches wide. Use one of these pieces for the bottom section of the holder. Refer to Fig. 3-13 for the various dimensions of these pieces

and for the way the side and bottom pieces fit together. Save the other 10-inch piece for the back strips.

[3] A curved area needs to be cut out on the top section of both side pieces. Refer to Fig. 3-13 for some dimensions that will assist you in cutting these areas. After measuring and marking the side pieces, cut out the curved areas using a saber saw.

[4] For the top section of the holder, cut another piece that is 10 inches long from the 1-×-6 board. Depending upon the area where you plan to hang the holder, you can vary the width of the top piece. As Fig. 3-13 suggests, the top piece should be at least 4 inches wide.

To make sure that the curved sides are the same, you should make a pattern from construction paper. It's worth the extra effort to make a pattern for these kinds of projects. You want an exact, well-balanced top piece where the curves are the same.

Pattern and cut the piece using a saber saw. The ends of the top piece should be at least 1¾ inches wide.

Fig. 3-12. Hanging Telephone Book Holder.

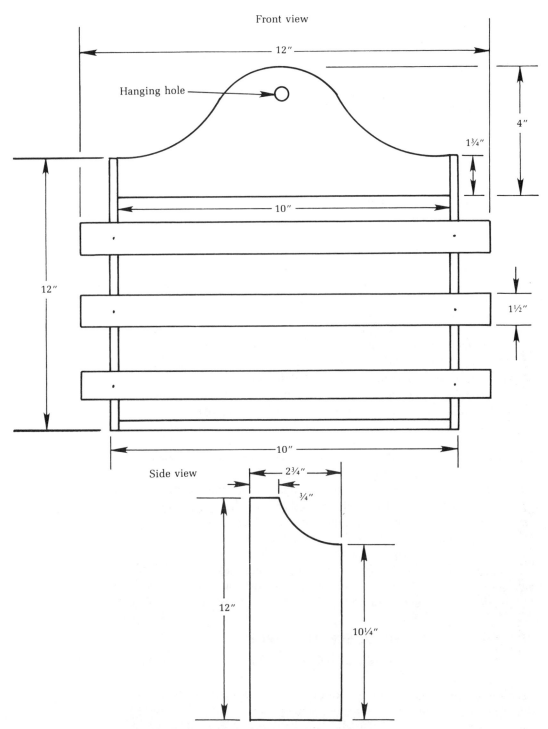

Front view

12″

Hanging hole

4″

1¾″

10″

12″

1½″

10″

Side view

2¾″

¾″

12″

10¼″

Fig. 3-13. Front and side views of the Hanging Telephone Book Holder.

[5] Measure and mark the center of the top piece and drill a ¼-inch-diameter hole in the upper section. This hole is for hanging the holder. Be certain it is in the center so the holder hangs straight.

[6] To make the front strips of the holder, cut another piece of the 1-×-6 material to a length of 12 inches. This length will permit the strips to slightly extend beyond the outer surfaces of the side pieces. Using either a band saw or the saber saw with a guide, rip three 1½-inch-wide strips from the 12 inch board. As Fig. 3-13 indicates, the holder has three front strips secured to its front.

[7] Back strips that fit inside the two side pieces also need to be cut. Since you already have one 10-inch-long piece that is 2¾ inches wide, you need not cut additional material for the back strips. (This 10-inch-long piece was the result of cutting the bottom piece in Task 2.)

Using the band saw or saber saw with its guide, rip the 10-inch-long piece into three strips that are approximately ¾ inch wide. The strips will not be exact in their width, but that's acceptable for their purposes. The strips will simply prevent the telephone directory or magazines from falling out the back of the holder as they are placed in it.

[8] Prior to assembly, rout the edges of the various parts using a round-over bit and a table-mounted router. It is not necessary to rout the back edges of the front strips. Do not over-rout the edges.

[9] Using a range of abrasive grits, sand all the surfaces and edges to finishing readiness. Be certain to sand with the grain of the wood.

[10] Assemble the holder using several sizes of finishing nails and wood glue. First, assemble the top piece, the two sides, and the bottom piece. Refer to Fig. 3-13 to note how the various parts fit together. Be certain that the top piece is securely attached to the inside of the side pieces. Allow the glue to dry before proceeding further.

[11] Attach the three front strips to the edges of the side pieces. Place the top strip at the bottom edges of the curved area on the side pieces. The bottom strip should cover the bottom piece of the holder. Center the middle strip between the other two strips. Remove any excess glue.

[12] Place the three 10-inch-long strips inside the two side pieces and flush with their back edges. Stagger them along the back edges. As indicated, they are designed to prevent books or magazines from falling out the back of the holder. Place them accordingly. Glue and nail in place.

PROJECT 7: SCROLL MIRROR

The Scroll Mirror (Fig. 3-14) presents a decorative frame that houses a standard piece of mirror glass. As the name suggests, the design consists of a series of scroll cuts around the outer edges of the frame. The frame is sufficiently large to provide ample surface for tole painting.

This design and subsequent mirror projects all use standard 12-×-12 mirror glass, which is available at most hardware stores. The mirror glass is usually of an excellent quality and a thickness that is easily cut. You will find it very effective for your various projects requiring mirror glass.

Although you might want to modify the size of the present project, the design is very functional. The mirror is of a size that can actually be used. In your planning activities, explore possible locations for a functional mirror of the size and design presented here. You might want to make a number of these mirrors once you identify areas in the household where they would be useful.

Figure 3-15 presents the frame, along with its dimensions. It also presents the approximate dimensions for the oval area in which the mirror glass is placed.

[1] You will need at least a 12-inch-long piece of 1-×-10 material. Recall that a 1-×-10 board is 9¼ inches wide. Thus, the frame has been designed to the actual width of the board. This is an example of how you can maximize your wood by designing projects around standard dimensions.

Because it is rather difficult to buy only 12 inches of a board, you might want to consider purchasing an 8- or 10-foot board. A number of later projects require 1-×-10 stock. Also, you might want to consider making more than one scroll mirror.

Measure and cut a piece of 1-×-10 material to a length of 11 inches.

[2] It is imperative that you make a pattern for this project. You will find it almost impossible to draw the various scrolls on the board's surface

Fig. 3-14. Scroll Mirror.

and have them all relatively even and similar in appearance. In addition to a pattern for the outer edges of the frame, you also need to make an oval pattern.

To make a pattern for the frame, you need to tape two pieces of construction paper together in order to obtain the proper width. As a rule, construction paper is 8½ × 11 inches. You need to add to the width of the pattern material so that it will be exactly 9¼ inches wide. Prepare the pattern material to a width of 9¼ inches and a length of 11 inches.

Fig. 3-15. Dimensions for the Scroll Mirror.

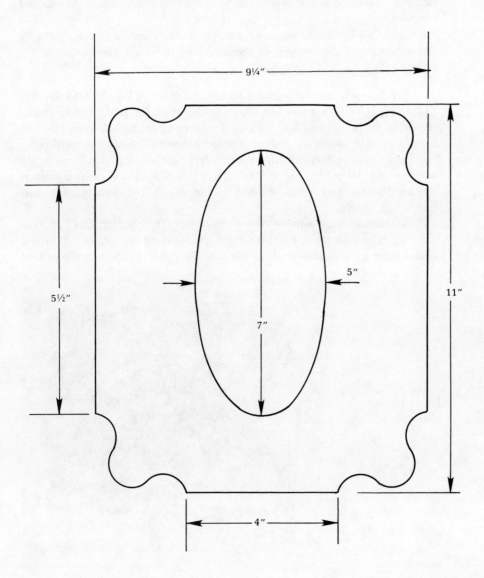

To make the various scrolls on the pattern, fold the pattern in half lengthwise. This procedure permits you to design one-half the pattern which, when cut, will be exactly duplicated on the other half. Refer to Fig. 3-15 for the length of the straight edges on the sides and also on the top and bottom. Mark the center of the pattern along the folded edge. This point will assist you in laying out the 5½-inch straight edge on the two sides. You will have 2¾ inches on both sides of the center line. Fig. 3-16 depicts this layout of the pattern, and should assist you in understanding the patterning procedure.

Place a mark 2 inches from the folded side on both the top and bottom edges of the pattern. These marks represent one-half of the 4-inch straight edge that is on the top and bottom of the frame. On the bottom corner of the pattern, draw a scroll that begins at the 2-inch mark and runs up to the 2¾-inch mark.

Refer to Fig. 3-16 to note the location of the scroll design. Take your time drawing the scroll design. Use a pencil so that you can erase the line easily. Draw the scroll until you're satisfied with its appearance.

[3] Using a pair of scissors, carefully cut out, along the pencil line, the scroll that you just made. You will use the piece that is cut out as the pattern for the upper corner, so handle it with care.

[4] Place the piece that was removed from the bottom corner at the top corner of the pattern. Trace the scroll on the pattern surface and cut with scissors. Open the folded pattern. You should have a perfect total pattern for the mirror frame. The scrollwork on all four corners should be exactly the same.

[5] You must also make an oval pattern. Although you could cut an oval from the frame pattern, it is easier to make a separate one. Again fold a piece of construction paper in half lengthwise. As Fig. 3-15 indicates, the oval should be at least 7 inches long and 5 inches wide. Mark the center of the paper on the folded edge. From the center point, measure 3½ inches both above and below it. Place a mark at both these points on the folded edge to get the length of the oval. Make a mark along the centerline exactly 2½ inches from the folded edge to get the width of the oval. Using a pencil, draw an oval that touches these three points.

You might find that an oval can be rather difficult to draw. Take your time until you have it right. If the process is too difficult, fold the pattern paper again, only this time fold it along the marked centerline. Draw what amounts to a quarter of an oval between the newly folded edge and the pencil mark along the initial folded edge. Using scissors, cut along the pencil line and open the paper. You should have a perfect oval.

While these pattern-making procedures can be somewhat frustrating, they are well worth the effort. Your projects are much more attractive and have a truly professional appearance about them when you use patterns. Practice the various procedures until you make a pattern that is acceptable.

[6] Trace the frame pattern on the 11-inch-long piece of 1-×-10 stock.

Take your time when tracing and be careful of the edges on the pattern. You might want to use the pattern again so try not to damage it.

[7] Using a saber saw and a fine-toothed blade, cut out the frame. Be certain to cut along the patterned line so the frame is an exact duplicate of the pattern. Don't be in a rush to finish the cutting function.

[8] Place the oval pattern on the frame and center it. Trace its outline on the wood's surface. Drill a ¼-inch-diameter hole through the inside area of the traced oval. Place the saber-saw blade in this hole to begin cutting the oval. Saw the oval out of the frame. Take your time with this function so that the oval is an exact duplication of the pattern.

[9] Rout the outside edges of the frame using a round-over bit and a table-mounted router. Rout both the front and the back edges. The back edge rout should be very slight. The front edge should have more of a rounded appearance than the back.

Fig. 3-16. Pattern for the Scroll Mirror.

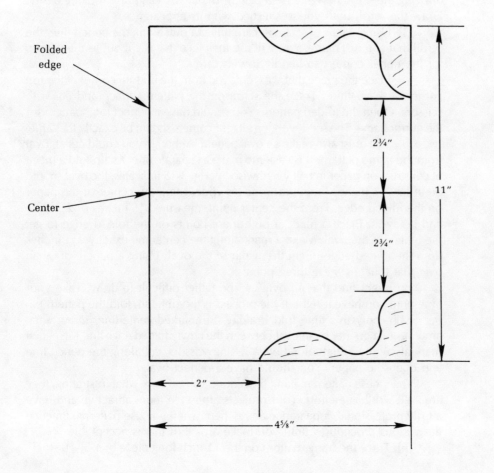

[10] You also need to rout the front edge of the oval with a round-over bit. Use the same bit setting as for the front edges. Do not rout the back edge of the oval with the round-over bit.

[11] In order for the mirror glass to be flush with the back surface of the frame, you must rout an area on the back surface of the oval. While a piece of mirror is often simply attached to the back surface of the frame, this is a shoddy way to make a mirror. It is best to set the mirror into the frame.

To rout the recessed area for the mirror glass, you will need a rabbeting bit and a table-mounted router. With the bit set to make a ⅛-inch-deep cut, rout the back area of the oval. Be certain you rout the back surface and not the front. To rout the recess, simply place the oval over the bit, bring its edge against the bearing of the bit, and rout. A depth of ⅛ inch is adequate to accommodate the thickness of standard mirror glass.

[12] For hanging the mirror on a nail, drill a tapered ¼-inch-diameter hole in the upper center of the back surface. You want to measure and mark this point so that the mirror will hang straight. Drill the hole to a depth of at least ⅜ inch, tapering it upward. Take your time so that you don't drill all the way through the frame.

[13] Sand the edges and the surfaces of the frame to finishing readiness. You will want to spend some time on this step so that you will have a good finish on the frame.

[14] If you are not inclined to cutting your own mirror glass, take your frame to a local glass shop. Most shops will cut the mirror glass to an exact fit. I hope, however, that you at least try to cut your own mirrors.

Before you begin the process of cutting the mirror glass, you need a pattern of the oval area and its recess. You will need to cut the glass so that it fits neatly into the recessed area. To make a pattern for the glass, trace an outline of the frame pattern on a piece of construction paper. Measure the width of the recess you made with the rabbeting bit. In most instances, this area will be ¼ inch wide. Using a ruler, make a series of marks on the pattern paper that are ¼ inch away from the edge of the traced pattern. You should mark all around the oval. The procedure is to draw a new oval by connecting these various marks with a pencil.

Cut the new oval from the construction paper and test it for fit in the recessed area of the frame. If it is too tight, remove some paper from the edge. It is better to have the pattern a bit too small than too large. This pattern will be the exact size of the mirror glass needed for the frame.

Most mirror glass is available in 12-×-12 panels. Using a felt-tipped pen, trace the oval mirror pattern on the reflecting surface of a panel. Use a fine-point pen and make the traced line dark enough so that it is easy to see and follow. It is best to place the pattern near one edge of the mirror panel to minimize waste. You should have sufficient glass remaining to make another scroll mirror or some other project.

To cut the mirror glass, you need a standard glass cutter (Fig. 3-17) and a steel edge ruler. Place a drop of household oil on the small wheel on the front of the cutter so that it rotates with ease. Every now and then, repeat this procedure.

[15] To cut glass, hold the cutter firmly in your hand and run the wheel over the line or area you want cut. The wheel lightly scores the surface of the glass and makes it possible to separate the glass along the scored line. You must use the cutter with both pressure and confidence. Only one firm pass should be made with the cutter along the marked line.

It is interesting to note how many people seem afraid to cut glass or mirror glass. This fear seems more related to breaking the glass than cutting themselves. For what it's worth, fear not. Mirror glass is relatively inexpensive and it is no great loss if you break a piece or cut it wrong. The chances of cutting yourself are very remote, at least if you are somewhat careful. After you score a few pieces and then separate them, you will find that glass cutting is really quite fun. It is interesting to see the various angles that can be cut.

Take a piece of mirror glass and make some practice cuts and then separate the pieces. As with anything else, you will need to practice the procedure a few times. Waste some mirror on yourself. Consider it an investment in learning.

Before you begin to cut the traced oval, separate the glass panel. Place the metal ruler near the edge of the traced oval. While you are holding the cutter firmly in your hand and at a slight angle, run the wheel down the glass, keeping the edge of the cutter against the ruler. Keep the pressure constant on the wheel. Place the scored line over the edge of a board or your workbench. While holding one part firmly against the surface, press down on the other part of the mirror. It should neatly separate along the scored line. Don't be afraid to give it some good, quick pressure. It is important that the scored line be directly over the edge of the surface of the board or bench. Save the extra piece for your next mirror project.

Incidentally, when you are cutting glass, be certain the area under the glass is flat and clean. You want the glass to lay perfectly flat against the surface when you are cutting. Also, remove any glass particles that remain from earlier glass cutting. These small particles can scratch the black coating on the back of the mirror panel. Scratches can be seen from the reflecting side of the mirror.

To cut the traced oval on the panel, the glass cutter needs to score along the inside edge of the traced line. You should score only one-half of the oval with each pass of the cutter. Place the cutter wheel at the top edge of the oval and, while applying pressure, slowly follow the traced line down to the bottom of the oval. Turn the panel around and repeat the process on the other side of the oval. Don't try to separate the pieces yet.

[16] In examining the glass cutter, you no doubt noticed two or three small grooves in the midsection of the cutter. These grooves are used for

Fig. 3-17. Glass cutter (courtesy of Red Devil, Inc.).

separating pieces of scored glass and also for chipping glass off the edges. Note that the grooves are of different widths. These widths are designed to fit over glass of different thickness. In addition to these grooves, note how the end of the glass cutter's handle is made into a partial ball. This weighted end is used to tap along the scored line to make separating the glass easier. You should not tap on the piece that is being cut. Tap only on the waste side of the scored line.

While holding the scored oval in one hand and holding the glass over a surface, tap along the scored lines. Next, place the groove that best fits over the edge of the mirror glass. Twist the glass cutter. A portion of the glass that surrounds the oval should separate immediately. Continue this procedure until all the excess glass is removed from the oval. Chip off any small, sharp edges that remain on the oval using the cutter groove. If you break the oval during these procedures, simply start over.

[17] Place the oval mirror in the recessed area of the frame and check for fit. It it is too large, use the cutter groove to chip away at the edges of the glass until it does fit. Take your time and keep chipping until you have a good-fitting mirror.

[18] Do not glue the mirror in place until after you have finished the frame with whatever products you plan to use. Use white glue to glue the mirror in place. Spread small dabs of glue along the mirror edge and the wall of the recess. Allow the glue to dry. To cover the mirror and its recess, measure and cut a piece of construction paper that will cover the entire back of the frame. Spread glue along the edge of the paper and press it in place. If you cover the hanging hole with the paper, simply punch a hole in the paper to expose the nail hole for hanging.

PROJECT 8: RECTANGULAR MIRROR

This project is for a large, functional mirror that can be placed and used in almost any room (Fig. 3-18). Although it is an attractive design, the project's focus is on function. It contains a rather sizable oval mirror that makes it effective for everyday use. Frequently mirror projects are used as decorative pieces at the expense of function. This project seeks to eliminate this conflict.

Unlike the Scroll Mirror, this project is relatively easy to make. You will need to make a pattern for the oval cutout in the frame, as well as to cut the mirror glass. More about this shortly. Figure 3-19 depicts the mirror design and its dimensions. You will find it helpful to refer to Project 7 while making this project.

[1] The frame for this design is made from 1-×-10 material. If you want an even larger mirror, consider using 1-×-12 stock. Recall that a 1-×-10 board is 9¼ inches wide, and a 1-×-12 one is 11¼ inches wide. Note, however, that the wider boards are more prone to warping. The board can place

sufficient stress on the mirror glass during the warping process and actually break it. This is an unusual occurrence, but it does happen. In any event, measure and cut the frame to a length of 12 inches.

[2] In order to have an attractive and even oval cutout for the mirror, you need to make a pattern. The oval should be near perfect, or it will distract from the overall project. As indicated in Fig. 3-19, the oval should be at least 9 inches long and 6 inches wide. Use a piece of construction paper for the pattern. Refer to Project 7 for the specific procedures to make an oval pattern.

[3] After you prepare the pattern, center it on the frame and trace its outline. Drill a ¼-inch-diameter hole inside the outline to enable the saber-saw blade to begin its cutting function. Carefully cut out the oval.

[4] Rout the edges of the frame and the front edge of the oval using a round-over bit. Do not rout the back edge of the oval with the round-over bit. Refer to Project 7 for a discussion of the routing tasks. Also, note the procedure for making a hanging hole in the back surface.

[5] Rout a recess in the back surface of the oval to hold the mirror glass. As noted in Project 7, a rabbeting router bit is used to make the recess. Follow the various procedures presented with that project.

[6] When the routing function is completed, sand the edges and surfaces of the frame to a finishing readiness. The frame needs to be finished completely

Fig. 3-18. Rectangular Mirror.

before you secure the mirror in place. A piece of construction paper is an effective way to cover the entire back of the frame. Glue it to the frame using white glue.

[7] Prior to cutting the oval mirror for the frame, make a pattern that is the exact size of the mirror needed. Project 7 presents a detailed discussion on preparation of the mirror pattern, and on mirror glass and using a glass cutter. Refer to these discussions to complete this project.

Fig. 3-19. Dimensions for the Rectangular Mirror.

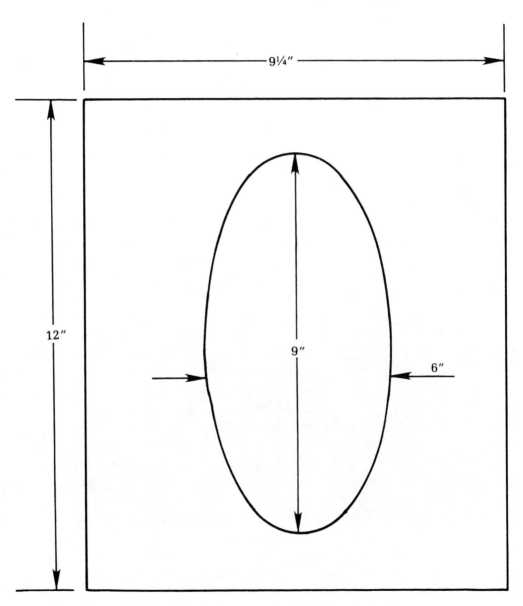

PROJECT 9: HAND MIRROR

The Hand Mirror project (Fig. 3-20) is both fun and somewhat challenging to make. As you will discover, the handle, frame, and center area can test your skill with a saber saw. It can be difficult, initially, to cut a perfect circle with a saber saw. It's one of those tasks, however, that can be done if you take your time. Much of the process has to do with simply concentrating on the patterned line as you cut along it. More about this shortly.

Another challenging part of this project is to cut a perfect circle of mirror glass that will fit into the frame recess. Although you can cut the circle with a standard glass cutter, as presented in Project 7, you might want to obtain and use a circle glass cutter (Fig. 3-21). In some ways, cutting a circle of glass with the circle glass cutter is much easier than cutting with a standard cutter. I will provide some instructions on the use of this device in the cutting step.

This project results in a piece that is both functional and decorative. The mirror diameter is of a size that can actually be used. I generally drill a hole in the handle and thread a piece of leather shoelace through it for hanging the project. The lace makes it possible to hang the mirror on a peg of one of your Shaker peg boards. It adds a nice touch to the peg board.

Fig. 3-20. Hand Mirror.

Although there is not a great deal of surface on the frame, the handle and lower section of the mirror area do present some surface for tole painting. No doubt some decorative design could be used to enhance the entire piece. Figure 3-22 presents a drawing of the project, along with its dimensions.

[1] The project requires a piece of 1-×-8 stock that is approximately 12 inches long. This length gives you an extra 1 inch of board that makes both patterning and sawing easier. As shown in Fig. 3-22, the width of the frame is 6¼ inches. While it does make for some waste of material, the design seemed best suited to this final width. You might want to increase both the length and the width of the project, not only to have a larger mirror area, but also to maximize your material. Cut the stock to the suggested length.

[2] You will definitely want to make a pattern for the mirror frame. It is almost impossible to draw the frame freehand and have it look acceptable. To match the various curves and keep the lines of the frame uniform would be difficult to do directly on the board's surface. Thus, it is best to make a pattern.

Use a piece of construction paper for making the pattern. It's best to use the pattern method described in Project 7. Laying out half the design on a folded piece of paper is a most effective method of pattern-making.

Trace the finished pattern on the board's surface and cut using a saber saw and a fine-toothed blade. Take your time with the sawing function to that the sides are equal and the edges are clean. Follow the pattern line with the blade.

[3] There are a number of devices for drawing a 4-inch-diameter circle in the center of the frame. One inexpensive and effective device is to use a school compass. Locate the center of the frame using a ruler. Set the diameter of the compass, place the point at the center location, and draw the circle.

Another device for making circles is the bottom of a can. I often use coffee cans, quart paint cans, or any other type of can that approximates the

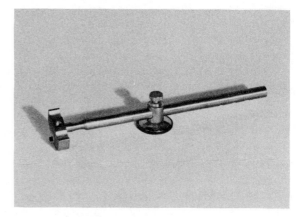

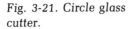
Fig. 3-21. Circle glass cutter.

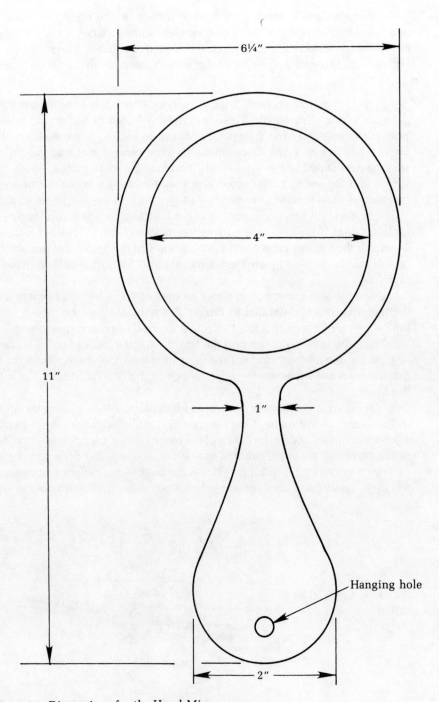

Fig. 3-22. Dimensions for the Hand Mirror.

72

diameter needed. The can need not be the exact diameter required for a given project. Nothing in woodworking needs to be that precise. A can that has a diameter of approximately 4 inches is more than adequate.

[4] To cut the circle area out of the frame, drill a blade hole inside the pattern lines. Place the saber-saw blade through the hole and begin cutting. Take your time. Concentrate on the circle line as you move the blade into the wood. Keep the saw steady and its base tight against the surface of the board. It is comforting to remember that if something does go wrong with the cut, you can always use sandpaper to clean it up.

[5] Drill a ¼-inch-diameter hole through the top center of the handle. If you prefer not to have a hanging hole, omit this procedure.

[6] As always, you need to rout the edges of the frame, both front and back, so they are round. Also rout the front edge of the mirror area. Do not rout the back edge, and do not rout off too much wood. The edges only need to be slightly rounded to enhance the overall appearance of the project. Frequently, there's a tendency to over-rout edges on projects.

[7] In order to have the mirror glass properly placed in the frame, you must rout a recessed area in the back surface. This procedure is best done using a rabbeting bit on a table-mounted router. The recess should be approximately ⅛ inch deep. Refer to Project 7 for procedures on how to rout the mirror recess.

If you want the mirror to be recessed further into the frame, simply rabbet the area to the desired depth. Do not set the rabbetting bit to make the deeper cut in one pass. Make several passes with the bit at different settings. To make a deep cut in one pass can be dangerous. Use your router with care and with the guidance of the owner's manual.

[8] Sand the surfaces and edges to finishing readiness.

[9] As suggested, cutting a round piece of glass is not all that complicated if you use a circle glass cutter. Set the cutter to the radius (half the diameter) of the piece of glass needed. Measure to the edge of the mirror recess and not just the diameter of the circle. It is one-half of this dimension that must be used in setting the cutter.

To set the cutter, loosen the adjustable suction cup. Measure from the edge of the cutting wheel to the center of the suction cup, and lock the suction cup in place when it is at the exact measurement. A good procedure for this process is to hook the cutter wheel over the edge of a metal ruler and slide the suction cup down the face of the ruler. Stop when the center edge of the cup is at the exact point on the ruler that is needed. Twist the cup screw tightly in place.

Before you place the cutter on the glass, wipe off any dust that has gathered on the face of the mirror. If the glass surface is not clean, the suction cup will not hold, but will slide on the surface. Spread saliva on the bottom surface of the suction cup. Use one hand to press and hold the cup against the glass, and with the other hand, rotate the cutter wheel end in a complete circle.

As with a standard glass cutter, keep pressure constant on the cutter wheel as you move it in a circle. It needs to score the surface of the glass.

Although using the circle cutter seems terribly awkward at first, the procedure does get easier. It is critical that you do not allow the suction cup to slide on the glass surface. If you do, you will cut an oval or some other odd shape, rather than the desired circle. Keep the suction cup under constant pressure when you are moving the cutting arm over the glass.

[10] To remove the scored circle from the glass panel, it is best to use a standard glass cutter. Using a ruler and the cutter, separate the circle piece from the unused mirror glass. With the heavy end of the cutter, tap along the scored circle. Tap on the outside area of the circle. This procedure should remove some of the glass surrounding the scored area. With the chip recess in the cutter, remove the remaining glass that surrounds the circle. Refer to Project 8 for a discussion of some of these cutting and chipping procedures.

[11] Place the mirror in the frame recess and check for fit. If it is too large, chip away some glass from its edge. Take your time with this procedure so you don't break the mirror. Continue the procedure until the mirror fits properly into the recess.

[12] Do not secure the mirror in the frame until you have done the finishing of the frame. Then glue in the mirror and place a piece of construction paper over the back surface.

PROJECT 10: PIG MIRROR

This project is an example of what can be done with animal shapes and mirror glass (Fig. 3-23). In addition to being decorative and different, the project is of a size that the mirror is usable. While you may prefer a design other than a pig, the project does demonstrate what is possible and how to make some unusual projects.

Although the design requires two patterns and some rather careful cutting with the saber saw, it is a fun and worthwhile project. Animal mirrors are a delight in a child's room. You might want to design a different animal or a bird of a size that will accommodate the same design for the internal mirror area. As the pig project demonstrates, you need only reduce the size of the frame design to dimensions that will fit inside the frame. More about this process will be given in the various tasks for the project.

Figure 3-24 presents an outline of the project, as well as its various dimensions. You might want to increase these dimensions if you prefer a larger frame and mirror. Do some design work before you begin the project.

[1] You will need at least an 11-inch-long piece of 1-×-8 material for the project. This length provides a little extra material to make the patterning and sawing functions easier.

[2] A pattern needs to be made for both the frame and the internal mirror area. Designs of this type simply must be drawn freehand on a piece of

construction paper and then cut. Refer to Fig. 3-24 for the various dimensions. You can refer to Project 18, Pig Cutting Board, for the pattern for the mirror frame. You will need to reduce its length, but it will be an excellent guide in the pattern-making process.

Use your imagination in drawing patterns for any project. You might want a different style tail or snout on the pig design. Modify the ears or any other portion of the pig to meet your own tastes. Make the pattern based on your perception of a pig and the way you want the frame and mirror area to look. Much of the fun of these projects is making patterns designed the way you want the final project to appear. Take advantage of the opportunity.

[3] When the frame pattern is finished, trace it on the 11-inch-long piece of 1-×-8 material. Using a saber saw and a fine-toothed blade, cut out the frame. Take your time and concentrate on cutting along the pattern line.

[4] After the frame has been cut, center the mirror pattern and trace it on the frame's surface. Drill a ¼-inch-diameter hole inside the pattern area. This hole is for the saber-saw blade so that the pattern area can be cut out. Very carefully, cut out the patterned mirror area. This is a much smaller area than the overall frame, so take your time when cutting. Again, concentrate on cutting along the pattern line.

[5] While the ¼-inch-diameter bit is still in a tool, drill a hanging hole in the back surface of the frame. Measure and mark the location of the hole so that the frame hangs straight. Slightly taper the drilled hole upward so that it will hang properly on a nail. Take your time drilling so you don't penetrate the front surface of the frame.

[6] Rout the edges of the frame round using a table-mounted router and a round-over bit. Also, rout the front edge of the mirror area. Do not rout the back edge of the mirror area with the round-over bit.

Fig. 3-23. Pig Mirror.

[7] In the back surface around the edges of the cutout area, rout a recess to hold the piece of mirror. The area should be routed to a depth of at least ⅛ inch using a ¾-inch-diameter straight-face router bit. This type of bit is also referred to a *mortise* bit. Set the bit to a cutting depth of no more than ⅛ inch. This depth is adequate for accommodating the mirror glass. Also, if the depth of cut is any deeper, the procedure becomes dangerous.

To rout the mirror area in the back of the frame, place the frame hole over the revolving bit. While you are holding the frame very tight, move it into the bit and rout out an area all around the mirror hole in such a way that a rectangular piece of glass can be cut and placed in the recess. You want to avoid the need to cut details of the pig from the mirror glass. This is almost impossible. Rout the recessed area to a shape that makes cutting and placement of the mirror simple.

[8] Using a range of abrasive grits, prepare the surfaces and edges for the finishing process. As indicated earlier, do not glue the mirror in place until the frame has been completely finished. Then glue the mirror to the recessed area using white glue. Cut a piece of construction paper to size and then glue it on the back surface of the frame. This gives the back a very finished appearance.

[9] To cut the mirror glass, measure the length and width of the routed recess. Mark these dimensions on a panel of glass and cut the mirror using a regular glass cutter. Refer to Project 7 for a discussion on cutting glass.

Fig. 3-24. Dimensions for the Pig Mirror.

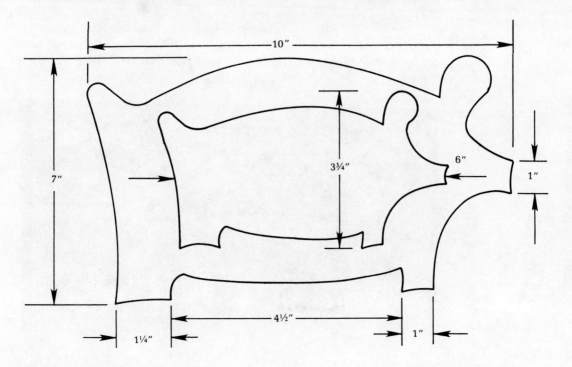

PROJECT 11: SINGLE TOWEL BAR WITH SHELF

This project includes a shelf surface for storage or display (Fig. 3-25). It is a very functional design for use in either a bath or kitchen. Generally, the shelf is made from 1-×-6 material. This width minimizes the space occupied by the unit, yet provides sufficient surface for folded hand towels or decorative pieces. The design includes a support piece to provide a means of securing the unit to the wall. It is always best to firmly secure units that will be used for towels to the wall.

The support piece on a shelf generally provides the means for hanging the shelf on the wall. It also makes the shelf top and legs sturdier because it ties them together. Another purpose of the support piece is to make the entire shelf more attractive. Generally, the support piece will be from 4 to 6 inches shorter than the shelf top. This length allows for a 2- or 3-inch overlap between the edge of the shelf top and the legs, on both sides. As a rule of thumb, the longer the shelf, the more the shelf top should overlap the legs.

The support piece should be *flush*, or even, with the outside edge of the legs. Generally, I use standard 1-inch-thick material and make the support piece 1¼ inches wide. These dimensions, especially on a shelf that will carry considerable weight, are usually adequate. On smaller shelves or those that will support only a minimum of weight, I rip the support piece to an approximate thickness of ½ inch. Hopefully, you will have some scrap lumber from which you can cut the support pieces, and you will not need to cut into new material.

Fig. 3-25. Single Towel Bar with Shelf.

You might want to use a ¾-inch-diameter dowel for the towel bar. This diameter makes for a more attractive project, but it also provides ample strength for continuous use. I usually extend the dowel through the shelf legs by at

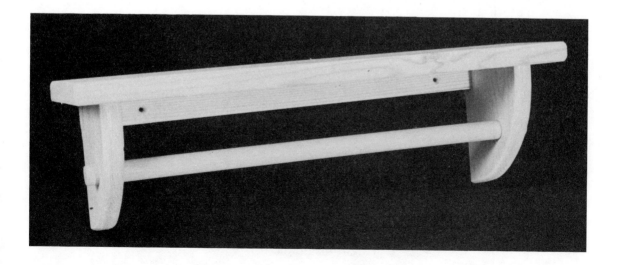

least 1 inch. The shelf itself should overlap the legs by at least 2 inches. This combination of overlapping pieces gives the project an attractive appearance.

Figure 3-26 presents one of the shelf legs and its approximate dimensions. Of course, you might want to significantly redesign the shape of the leg. Allow a minimum of 2 inches between the dowel and the bottom surface of the shelf top. Anything less makes it rather difficult to hang a towel on the bar.

Determine your location for the shelf and then design it to the dimensions needed. One of the significant advantages of making your own shelves is that you can custom-design and build them. Normally, you are very limited when buying a shelf. Do some planning before you decide upon both the design and the dimensions needed. To assist you in learning how to make the project, a 20-inch-long shelf will be used for the example.

[1] You will need sufficient 1-×-6 stock for the shelf, two legs, and a support piece. You can cut the support piece from any scrap that is the appropriate length. On a shelf 20 inches long, I plan to have the shelf top overlap the legs by at least 1½ inches on each side. Therefore, the support piece should be 17 inches long.

In addition to the pine boards, you will also need a ¾-inch-diameter dowel that is at least 19 inches long. The design anticipates that the dowel will extend

Fig. 3-26. Shelf leg design.

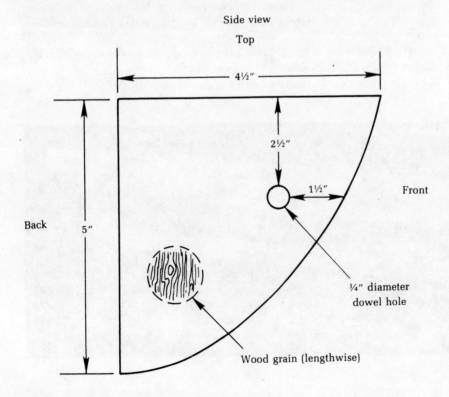

Side view

Top

Back

Front

4½"

2½"

1½"

5"

¾" diameter
dowel hole

Wood grain (lengthwise)

at least 1 inch beyond the outer surface of both legs. I find that by extending the dowels beyond the legs, the overall appearance of the shelf is greatly improved. Very often shelves tend to look too plain unless the leg surfaces have some enhancement.

Measure and cut the shelf top to its 20-inch length. Also, measure and cut the support piece to a length of 17 inches. It should be at least 1¼ inches wide. If you are making the shelf to some other dimensions, measure and cut accordingly.

[2] You would be well advised to make a pattern for the legs. You might prefer to draw one leg freehand, cut it out, and use it to pattern the second leg. When laying out the leg pattern on a board, be certain to do it with the wood grain. You should also use one edge of the board as the back edge of the leg to simplify the squaring and cutting procedures. A scroll saw is very effective in making the rounded cut on the front edge of the example legs. Be certain to review the drawing of the leg and its dimensions in Fig. 3-26. Although you might prefer another design, the dimensions given are in good proportion to the shelf top.

[3] After you have cut the legs, drill a ¾-inch-diameter hole through each of them. The dimensions, as presented in Fig. 3-26, will allow you to properly place the dowel holes on the legs. The location specified will provide ample support for the dowel and also enough room between the shelf bottom and the dowel. Of course, you might want to modify these dimensions in relation to your leg design. In any event, drill the ¾-inch-diameter holes through the legs. Place a support scrap under the legs when drilling to prevent tear out as the bit exits the leg.

[4] The next component you need to measure and cut is the shelf support piece. Refer to Fig. 3-27 for the placement of the support piece. As indicated earlier, the length of the support piece will determine how much of an overlap will be on both edges of the top shelf. With a 20-inch-long shelf top, I generally have a 1½-inch overlap on each side. Thus, the support piece should be 17 inches long. If you are making a shelf of a different length, modify the length of the support piece accordingly.

Rather than waste 1-×-6 material, I generally cut the support pieces from 1-×-4 stock. To be effective, the piece should be at least 1¼ inches wide and the thickness of the stock. In laying out and measuring the support piece, use one edge of the board as one edge of the support piece. It is usually a good, straight edge and will save you some time and cutting. After you have cut the support piece to length and width, drill two holes through it using a countersink drill bit or similar device. The holes should be about 3 inches from each end of the support piece. These holes are for screws, nails, or whatever else you want to use to hang the shelf. Figure 3-27 presents the layout of the support piece on the board and also the finished component.

[5] In order to secure the two legs to the support piece, you must trace

and cut an area from the back of the legs. Place the end of the support piece against the side surface of a leg, flush with the top and back edge. Trace an outline of the support end onto the leg's surface. Follow this procedure for the other leg, as well.

Using a saber saw or a handsaw, carefully cut out the traced area from both legs. Cut on the penciled lines so that you will have a good fit when you assemble the support piece and leg. Be certain to support the leg on a solid surface during the cutting process.

[6] Rout the edges of the shelf top and legs using a table-mounted router. I use a ⅜-inch quarter round or round-over bit for this project. You may prefer using a ⅜-inch cove bit for a different profile. When I use a cove bit, I rout only the front and sides on the top area of the shelf and the front edges of the legs. Round the other edges using a quarter round bit. Be certain not to rout any edges that will abut other parts when assembled.

Do not rout the edges of the support piece. You want to leave the sharp edges of the support piece so that they will fit neatly into the cutout areas

Fig. 3-27. Support piece.

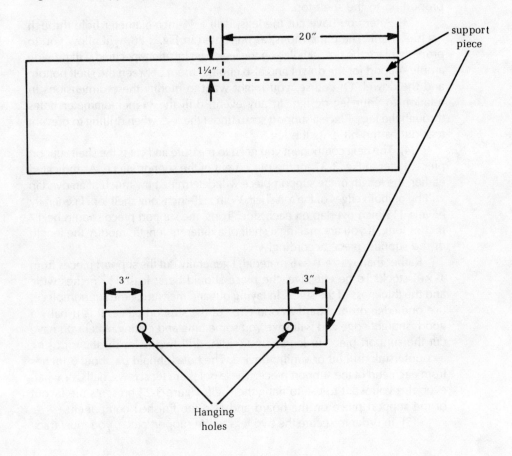

20"

1¼"

support piece

3"   3"

Hanging holes

of the legs. Rout the shelf top on all edges except the bottom edge that will rest on the support piece. You want to have sharp edges where the shelf top and support piece come together. Rout only the face edges of the legs and a portion of the back edges. Do not rout the top edges of the legs. Here, again, you want sharp edges where the legs will be attached to the bottom surface of the shelf top. On the back edges of the legs, I stop routing about ¼ inch below the support-piece cutouts so there are sharp edges for the attachment of the legs and support piece.

[7] Sand the routed edges, but do not sand the nonrouted edges of the various parts. You want to leave sharp and straight edges for assembly. Wear a dust mask when sanding.

[8] After you have finished sanding, wipe all surfaces with a rag. You want to remove any dust from areas that will be glued because dust prevents glue from doing its job. If you have an air compressor, use it for blowing away the accumulation of sawdust. A slightly dampened rag is also a good method for removing sawdust from the surfaces. Too much water on the rag, however, will stain the wood.

[9] The first assembling task is to join the two legs and the support piece. Using yellow wood glue, spread a bead on the two cut edges of a leg where the support piece will fit. Start two finishing nails in each end of the support piece, one above the other. Place the nails so that they will penetrate into the center portion of the leg. The two countersunk drill holes that you made in the face of the support piece should be facing out toward the front of the shelf. With the nails started and the glue spread, set the support piece in the leg cutout. Place the front edge of the leg against a hard surface and drive in the two nails. Be certain the edge of the support piece and the outer surface of the leg are flush before nailing. Also, be certain the leg is straight in relation to the support piece. You do not want to have a crooked leg under the shelf top.

Using a damp cloth, wipe off any excess glue that might squeeze out during this assembling procedure. The glue stains the wood, so you want to remove any excess from the surfaces. Also, wood stain does not cover glue that remains on the surface. It cannot penetrate into the wood through the glue. Remember, more glue is not better.

Repeat this assembly process with the other leg. If you have an air-powered nailer, this assembly procedure is very quick and easy. It is one of the many tasks that a pneumatic nailer does well.

Incidentally, you can use screws in place of finishing nails to secure the support piece to the legs, if you desire. Drill pilot holes through the support piece to receive the screws and then secure them to the legs. Screws will make for a much stronger shelf. When you are using screws, you also want to use wood glue.

[10] Insert the dowel into the leg holes and check for fit. Increase the

diameter of the holes, if necessary, using either abrasive paper or a round wood rasp or file. You want the dowel to fit snugly but not too tightly. If you force the dowel into the holes, there's a good chance the legs could split. The dowel should extend at least 1 inch beyond the outer surface of each leg. Place a touch of glue in each hole and align the dowel. Wipe off the excess glue with a warm, damp cloth. Allow the glue to dry.

[11] Before you assemble the legs and support assembly to the shelf top, be certain that the top edges of the legs and the support piece are flush. If they are not, sand them flush. You want the surfaces of the legs and support piece to make good contact with the bottom of the shelf piece. It not only looks better, but makes for a more secure shelf.

[12] Place the shelf piece, top face down, on a clean surface. Remember, you have sanded all the pieces so you do not want to get them dirty or scratched. Set the leg and support assembly, as it will be assembled, on the shelf piece. Mark the exact location of the leg assembly on the bottom surface of the shelf piece. The shelf top must overlap the same distance from each leg. Place the assembly flush with the unrouted bottom edge of the shelf piece. Using the dimensions of our sample shelf, the outer surface of the legs should be about 1½ inches from the edges of the shelf piece. You will need a ruler to make these measurements. When one end of the assembly is 1½ inches from the edge, the other should be also. Place small pencil marks on the surface of the shelf piece where each leg should be secured. Also, make marks on the back edge of the shelf piece at the same locations. You will use these marks for alignment when you secure the leg assembly and the shelf top together. Figure 3-28 depicts these procedures.

Fig. 3-28. Aligning the leg assembly and shelf top.

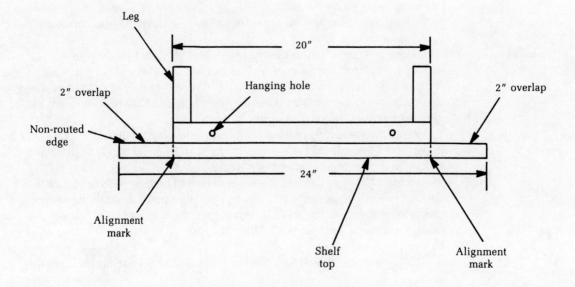

To assist you in nailing the shelf top to the leg assembly, you might want to mark points on the top surface of the shelf where the nails should be placed. Use the alignment marks on the back edge of the shelf piece as guides. Use a try square for this marking procedure. Be certain to place the nail marks ⅜ inch in from the alignment marks. Remember, the alignment marks are at the outer edge of the legs. By moving the nails in from these marks by ⅜ inch, you will place them directly over the center of the legs. Also, remember that the legs do not extend the entire width of the shelf top. I generally drive two finishing nails into each leg and three into the support piece. Figure 3-29 depicts the layout for nailing the shelf top to the leg assembly.

[13] Spread a bead of glue on the top surfaces of both legs and on the total length of the support piece. Smear the glue around with your finger. You will want to use extra glue on the legs because their surfaces are cross-grain. A cross-grain surface tends to absorb the glue more quickly, so you must use extra. Do not use too much glue on any of the surfaces, since it will squeeze out when you assemble the components. With the shelf top laying on a flat surface, bottom surface up, place the glued leg assembly between the alignment marks. Place it carefully so you do not smear glue around on the shelf surface. Be certain the back edge of the support piece is flush with the back edge of the shelf top. Press the assembly down and allow the glue to begin to dry.

Fig. 3-29. Nailing the leg assembly to the shelf top.

Top view

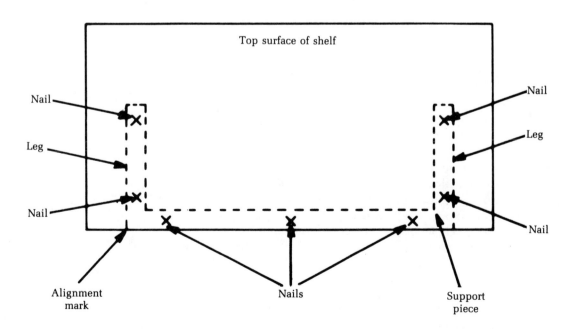

After the glue begins to set up, turn over the entire assembly carefully and stand it on the two legs. Although this procedure is somewhat awkward, it can be done. Drive the first finishing nail in at the center of the support piece. Be sure to drive the nail from the top surface of the shelf into the center of the support piece. You can drive the nail while the glued assembly rests against one hand. Drive the second nail into the end area of the support piece.

When these two nails are in place, the assembly will hold together and you can drive the remaining nails into the legs and the support piece. Check to see that the top edges of the legs are flush against the bottom surface of the shelf piece. If not, lightly tap them into place. If you are having problems nailing the shelf together, have someone hold the glued assembly while you drive in the nails. You also can use bar clamps to secure the leg assembly and shelf top while you are nailing them.

[14] After the nails are all in place, use a nail punch to drive their heads under the board's surface. If you are interested in production woodworking, these kinds of jobs are well suited for a pneumatic nailer. With an air-powered nailer, these types of assembling tasks can be done in a matter of seconds. The nailers also countersink the nails as they are driven into the boards.

PROJECT 12: MARBLE TOWEL HOLDER

Although a small project, the Marble Towel Holder (Fig. 3-30) is one of the more interesting and ingenious devices I've encountered. It lends itself as a project for both the kitchen or bath. The holder is so small and effective that a number of them can be placed in various locations in a room. Frequently they are secured to the sides of refrigerators, the ends of cabinets, near the range area, or anywhere else that a towel is needed. As you will discover, the holder can be secured with either a screw or double-face tape. The project is an excellent one for tole painting.

The towel holder works on the principle of a regular marble moving in a sloping trench. After the edge of a towel is slid into the unit, it is pulled downward. The marble forces it against the back surface of the front section of the holder and locks it in place. The more the towel is pulled downward, the tighter the hold. To remove the towel, it is simply pulled to the side. The marble immediately releases it. This simple principle that is reflected in the holder is one of those universal ideas of unknown origin. It is, however, extremely clever and effective as a towel holder.

Another good part of this project is that the dimensions are sufficiently small so it can be made from pine scraps. The project is made of two components that are easily assembled with glue and nails. The basic support backing is approximately 5½ inches long and 3 inches wide. The front section that holds the marble in the trench is 4¼ inches long and 2¼ inches wide. Figure 3-31 presents the front and side views of the holder, along with the appropriate dimensions.

As you will note in Fig. 3-31, the front section is partially sawed in half. It is critical to note and study the various dimensions of this front section. The ability of the towel holder to function properly depends upon this piece.

Figure 3-32 presents a side and front view of the marble trench. The trench must be routed into the support piece using a special hand-made jig. More about this shortly.

[1] Depending upon how many of these marble holders you want to make, cut out the support backing pieces to a length of 5½ inches and a width of 3 inches. The wood grain should run lengthwise on both the support backing and the front section. Measure and cut the front section to a length of 4½ inches and a width of 2¼ inches. Small projects are best cut on a band saw using a ½-inch-wide blade. You can, of course, cut the main components using a saber saw with a fine-toothed blade. Be certain that the width of the support piece is exact and standardized if you are preparing more than one holder. The hand-made routing jig is designed to accommodate only a 3-inch-wide support piece.

Using a fence on the band saw, rip the front section partially in half. Check the various dimensions of this cut in Fig. 3-31. These dimensions are critical to the smooth functioning of the unit. In order that the holder doesn't look

Fig. 3-30. Marble Towel Holder.

too much like a box, I cut the corners off the bottom of the front piece (Fig. 3-31). It greatly enhances the appearance of the holder.

[2] To rout the trench in the support backing piece, I use a ¾-inch-diameter mortise bit. This diameter is sufficiently wide to allow a standard marble to roll freely in the routed trench. The trench, as Fig. 3-32 indicates, is 2¼ inches long. It is ½ inch deep for approximately 1 inch at the top part of the trench. It then begins to slowly slope upward until it reaches the top surface of the support piece. The trench stops within ¼ inch of the bottom edge of the support piece. You can rout the entire trench with one pass of the router using the ¾-inch-diameter mortise bit.

Fig. 3-31. Side and front views of the Marble Towel Holder.

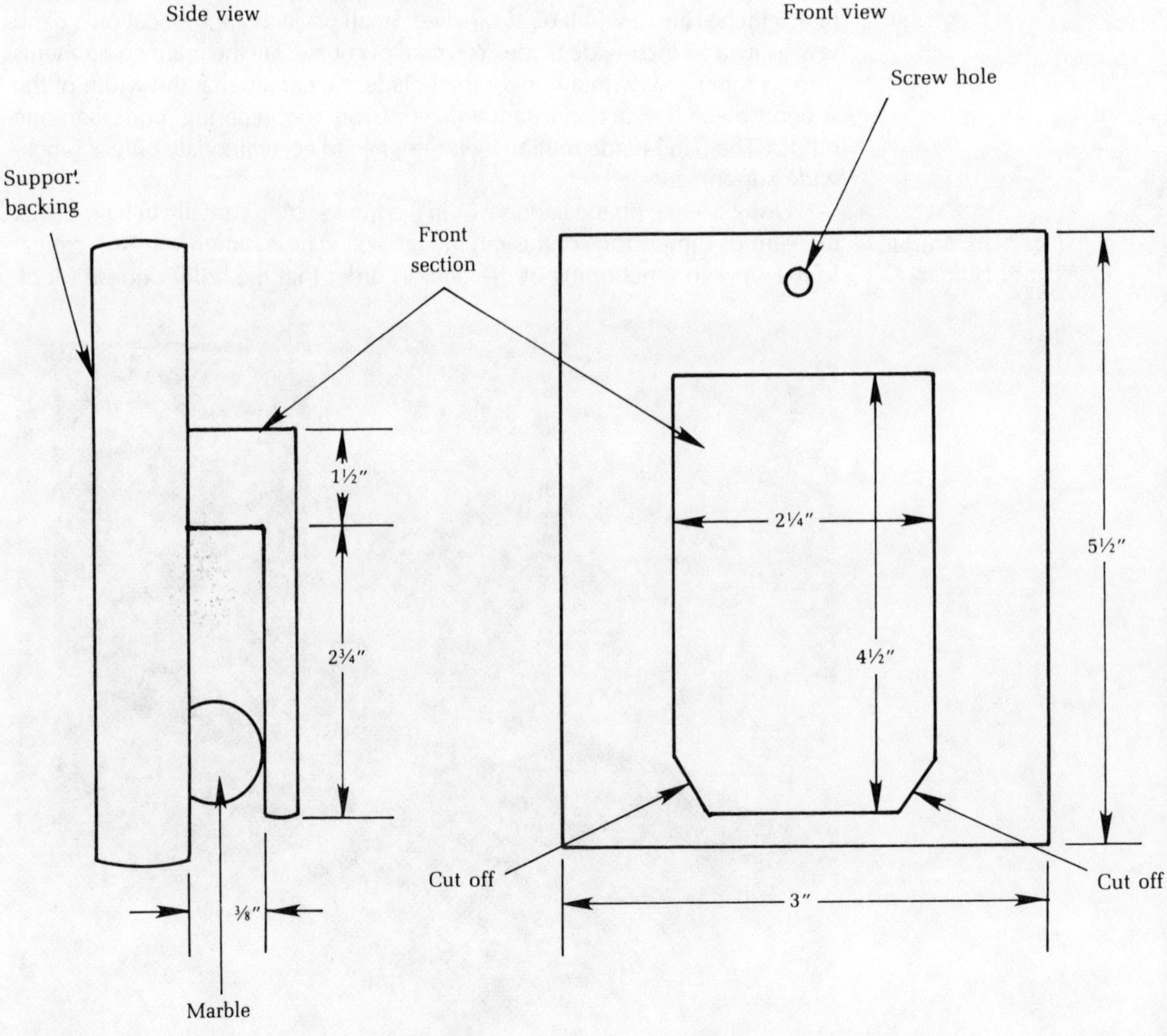

Side view

Front view

Screw hole

Support backing

Front section

1½"

2¾"

3⁄8"

Marble

2¼"

4½"

5½"

Cut off

Cut off

3"

Figure 3-33 presents a top view of a jig that I designed to hold the support piece while it is being routed. The jig also supports and guides the bottom of the router during the routing process. The side walls of the jig are designed to the diameter of the particular router base used. My jig was designed to accommodate a router with a 5¾-inch-diameter base. You should measure the base diameter of your router and modify the jig accordingly.

Figure 3-34 presents a front view of the jig with approximate dimensions. Slide the support backing piece between the ¼-inch-thick strips attached to the base of the jig. The fit should be snug so that the support is not pulled out during the routing procedure. As you will note, the area between the side walls is the diameter of the router base. I make this area a fraction larger so that the router base will move freely during the routing procedure.

To use the jig, place the support piece between the strips. Set the router bit to cut a ½-inch depth. Place the router between the side walls with the bit a fraction over the surface of the support piece. Start the rout ¼ inch from

Fig. 3-32. Routing the marble groove.

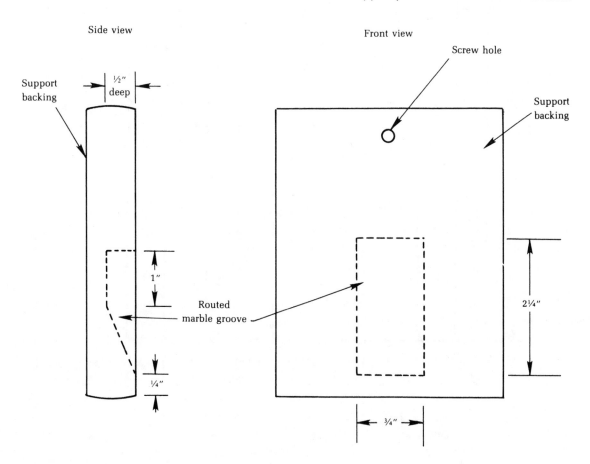

the bottom edge of the support. Turn the router on and make a sloping cut of approximately 1¼ inches and a flat cut of approximately 1 inch. Remove the router from the cut trench. The marble trench should be routed in one pass. If the jig tends to move during the routing process, you might want to

Fig. 3-33. Top view of the jig.

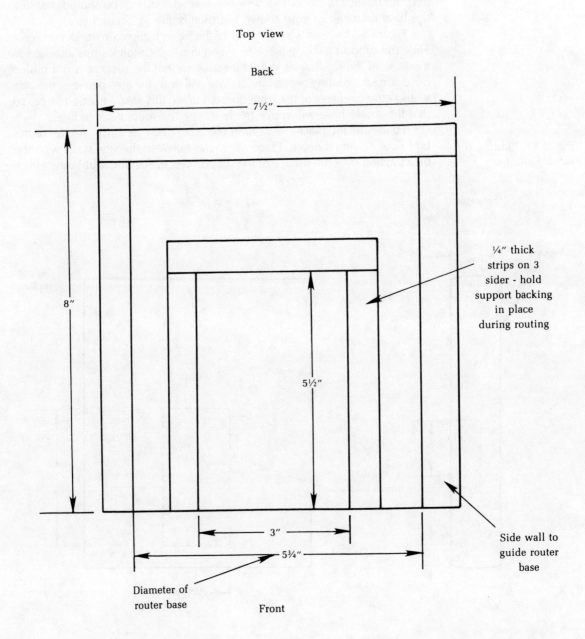

Top view

Back

7½"

8"

5½"

¼" thick strips on 3 sider - hold support backing in place during routing

Side wall to guide router base

3"

5¾"

Diameter of router base

Front

nail it to a surface. As always, use caution and effective safety procedures when using the router. Be certain to wear safety equipment.

[3] If you want to secure the towel holder using a screw or nail, drill a hole in the upper center of the support piece. You might prefer to use strips of double-faced tape placed on the back of the support piece for hanging. Refer to Fig. 3-31 for the approximate placement of the hanging hole.

[4] Rout, using a round-over bit, or sand the edges of both the support backing and the front piece. You should also sand all surfaces and bring them to a finishing readiness. For routing, I use a table-mounted router.

[5] Before you assemble the front piece to the support backing, place a standard marble in the routed trench. Spread glue on the back surface of the front piece that will attach to the front surface of the support piece. Center the front piece on the support and put it in place (Fig. 3-31). Allow the glue to partially dry and then nail, using finishing nails, from the back of the support. Be careful that the glued front piece doesn't move during the nailing process. You can, of course drive your nails in from the front surface of the front piece. When placed through the back, however, the nails don't show. Allow the assembly to dry before testing.

[6] To secure a towel in the finished holder, slide the hem edge of a towel up to the top of the front-piece groove. Allow the marble to drop behind the towel's edge. Pull the towel straight down to lock it in place. To remove the towel from the holder, pull it up and to the side of the unit.

Fig. 3-34. Front view of the jig.

Front view

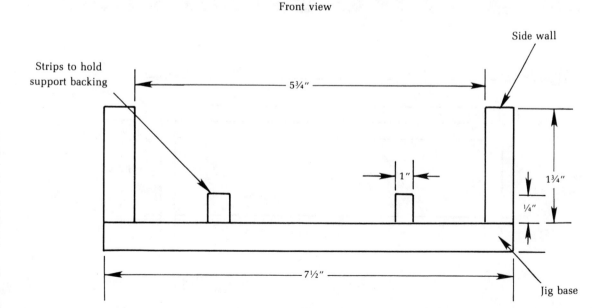

89

PROJECT 13: PAPER TOWEL HOLDER WITH SHELF

The Paper Towel Holder with Shelf (Fig. 3-35) presents a design that accommodates a large roll of paper towels, but also has a shelf for storage or display. A support piece is used in this design to better secure the unit to the wall. The unit needs to be securely fastened to a wall or everytime a paper towel is pulled from the roll, items on the shelf will fall off. The placement of the dowel is necessary to prevent the roll of toweling from rubbing on the support piece. Figure 3-36 presents the project, as well as some dimensions that you might want to use.

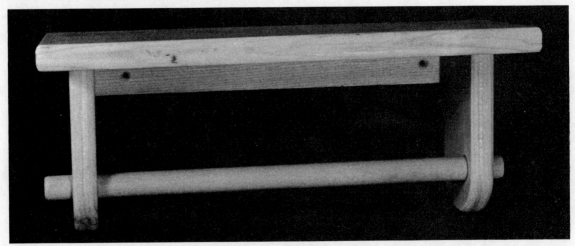

Fig. 3-35. Paper Towel Holder with Shelf.

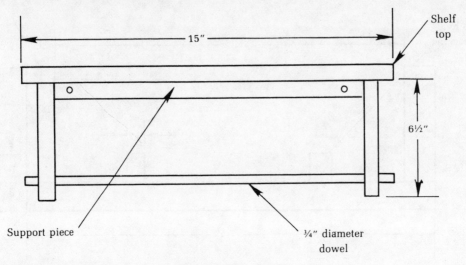

Fig. 3-36. Front view of the Paper Towel Holder with Shelf.

[1] The project requires 1-×-6 stock for the shelf top and 1-×-4 material for the legs. You can rip the support piece from scrap. A ¾-inch-diameter dowel is recommended. Using the 1-×-6 stock, measure and cut the shelf top to a length of 15 inches.

[2] The legs for the project are best prepared from 1-×-4 stock. Pattern or design the legs freehand to a length of 6½ inches and a width of 3½ inches. This width is the actual width of 1-×-4 material. Figure 3-37 depicts a leg, its dimensions, and the location of the dowel hole. As indicated, place the dowel toward the front edge of the legs on this design. This placement prevents the toweling from rubbing on the support piece or, with larger rolls, on the wall.

Side view

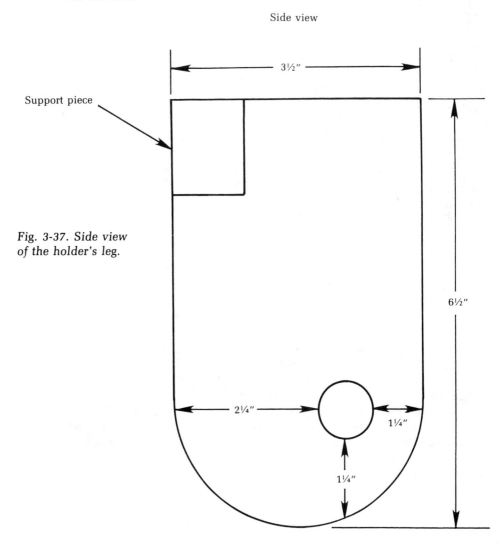

Fig. 3-37. Side view of the holder's leg.

Pattern and cut the legs. Using Fig. 3-37 as a guide, lay out the location of the dowel on each leg. Drill ¾-inch-diameter holes through both legs.

[3] Measure and cut the support piece to a length of 13 inches. It should be at least 1¼ inches wide, cut from standard thickness pine. Using this length for the support piece will allow the shelf top to overlap the legs by 1 inch on each side. If you are curious, this length was arrived at by adding the 11½-inch length required by the roll of toweling and the ¾-inch thickness of the two legs. With a 15-inch-long shelf top, this leaves a 1-inch overlap on each side. I generally limit the overlap on this design to minimize the amount of wall space required for the unit. You might prefer a long shelf top with a greater overlap. Drill two hanging holes in the support piece.

[4] Trace the butt end of the support piece onto the upper back surface of each leg (Fig. 3-37). Cut out the support area from both legs. A saber saw and fine-toothed blade work well for this procedure.

[5] If you have a table-mounted router, rout all edges using a ⅜-inch round-over or quarter-round bit. You might want to try a different edging bit for this design. I tend to use either a quarter-round or cove bit on most of the functional pine projects. There are, however, a range of other decorative router bits that you might want to consider.

Do not rout any edges that will be joined to another part during the assembly process. For example, do not rout the top edges of the legs because they will be attached to the bottom surface of the shelf top. If you do not have a router, use a small hand plane or abrasive paper to round the edges and corners.

[6] Cut a ¾-inch-diameter dowel to a length of 15 inches. This length will allow the dowel to extend beyond the surface of both legs by 1 inch. It will also match the shelf overlap.

[7] Using a range of abrasive papers, sand all the surfaces and edges to finishing readiness. It is much easier to do your sanding before the unit is assembled. You do, however, need to be careful with excess wood glue squeezing onto the newly sanded surfaces. Wipe off any excess glue using a warm, damp cloth.

[8] Using finishing nails and wood glue, assemble the support piece to the two legs. Next, assemble the shelf top to the leg assembly, being certain that there is a 1-inch overlap on both sides. Refer to Project 11 for a discussion of some of these assembling procedures.

[9] After the unit is assembled, test the fit of the dowel in the two leg holes. If necessary, widen the holes to accommodate the dowel. You want a snug, but not a tight, fit. It is best if the paper toweling rolls on the dowel. This will prevent the dowel from slipping out of a leg hole during use. Refer to Chapter 4 for a presentation of the finishing process.

PROJECT 14: DECORATIVE SHAKER PEG BOARD

This project is for a functional unit, but one that is somewhat decorative (Fig. 3-38). This project provides considerable surface for tole painting or other types of decorative work.

The project can be made to any length and width you desire. Also, the number of pegs is determined by how the unit will be used. Figure 3-39 presents one design you might want to consider. While dimensions are suggested, this type of project is best made based on your particular needs. Custom-design the project to fit a particular location. Most designs lend themselves to using either 1-×-6 or 1-×-8 stock.

While a rather basic scroll type design, the design shown in Fig. 3-39 looks good in any room. You might prefer designing and cutting the board with more scrollwork or some other type of detailed cutting. I tend to use rather simple designs that can be easily sawed for this type of project. You might prefer something that is more elaborate and that lends itself to a particular tole painting design. As always, a good practice is to make a pattern for tracing prior to sawing.

Another rather elementary design is shown in Fig. 3-40. This design demonstrates how the Shaker pegs can be staggered around the surface of the board. This approach to the placement of the pegs allows you to maximize the board for hanging decorative or functional items. It is critical that you place the pegs in relation to the size of the items that will be hung on them. Do some measuring as you plan your design.

Shaker peg boards can also be designed based on height. With the design

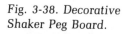

Fig. 3-38. Decorative Shaker Peg Board.

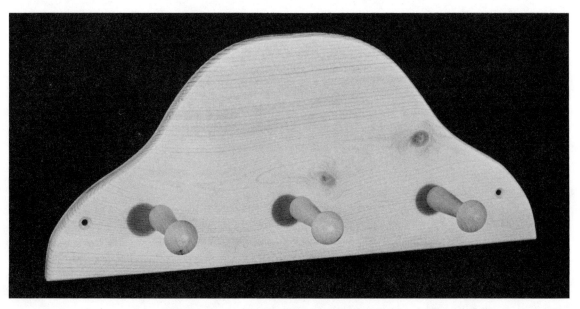

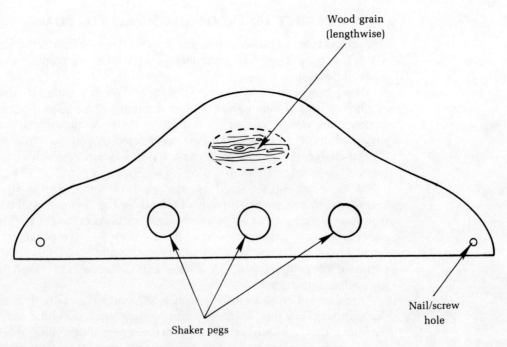

Fig. 3-39. *Front view of the Decorative Shaker Peg Board.*

Front view

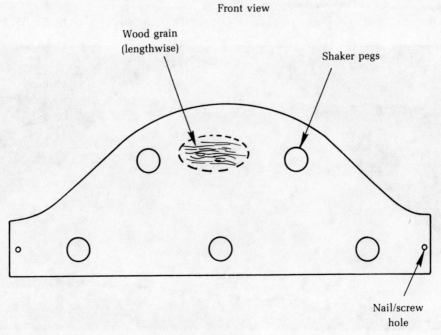

Fig. 3-40. *Decorative Shaker Peg Board with five pegs.*

presented in Fig. 3-41, a specific need should be identified. This type of design is primarily for displaying some item. Although it could serve some functional purpose as well, generally some decorative collection is displayed using this type of design. Approach the placement of the pegs on this design with care. You don't want displayed items too close to one another. Plan and measure carefully.

As you might guess, the possible designs for Shaker peg boards are almost endless. The pegs and their range of functions present you with many possibilities for decorative shapes and possible uses. You also can make designs that reflect the room they are placed in. You can also design themes

Fig. 3-41. Alternate design for the Decorative Shaker Peg Board.

Front view

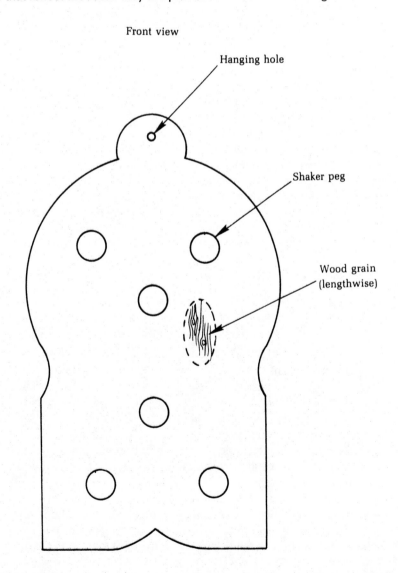

Hanging hole

Shaker peg

Wood grain
(lengthwise)

and objects—for example, music and baseball—into Shaker peg boards. How about a large musical note Shaker peg board or a baseball bat or glove Shaker peg board? Stretch your imagination and you will be delighted with the ways in which you can use these versatile pegs.

[1] Depending upon both the size and design of the backing, prepare and cut it as desired. You might want to measure the area to which you plan to secure the project, or at least have a general idea of the dimensions you want before you saw the unit. These dimensions might depend upon your planned use for the project, as well as a specific design you would like to paint on the backing.

[2] Measure and mark the location for the Shaker pegs or dowels. Using a ½-inch-diameter bit, drill the peg tenon holes through the backing. Always drill the holes from the front surface to the back. In this way, if tear-out does result from drilling, it will be on the back surface. Incidentally, most commercial Shaker pegs have a ½-inch-tapered tenon, so use a ½-inch-diameter bit.

[3] In order for the holder to be held securely to the wall, vanity, or other surface, you should make two nail/screw holes through the backing. Drill the holes through the surface, where they will give the backing the most support when secured. Any project using pegs should be securely attached to a surface. Chapter 4 provides both information and assistance on some of the various methods best used for hanging projects.

[4] Rout or sand the face edges of the backing. Also sand the surface and edge to finishing readiness.

[5] Spread glue on each Shaker peg's tenon and drive it into a ½-inch-diameter hole. Wipe off any excess glue. If the fit is not tight, squeeze some glue on the tenon edge from the back. Allow the glue to dry.

PROJECT 15: SMALL CABINET WITH DOOR

This project can hold a range of items from spices to collectibles or any number of other small items (Fig. 3-42). The cabinet has a hinged door with a large oval piece of glass in its center. The actual door is from a solid piece of wood, so it eliminates the need for making joints. If you prefer, you can use a solid door without glass. This option provides an opportunity to do some carving or painting on the door's surface.

The cabinet frame employs a simple butt joint, so it is relatively easy to make. While some cabinet frames and doors require mitered joints, this project can be done with minimal joinery skills. After you make the project, you will find that crafting cabinets with doors is a relatively uncomplicated process. The back of the cabinet can be made using either strips of pine or plywood.

Hardware for this type of project is readily available. You can purchase hinges that can be secured to the edge of the door frame and the outer surface of the cabinet frame to eliminate the need for chiseling or routing areas to accommodate hinges. You can also easily obtain either porcelain, metal, or wooden knobs for the door. They are generally available in a range of sizes and designs at local discount stores. Small catches or magnetic door catches also should be available locally. Generally, most stores stock a large variety of this type of hardware at reasonable prices. They are also available from any number of mail-order suppliers. Specifics on how to place the various hardware items are discussed in the tasks.

The large oval in the door requires a pattern of some kind. In addition to making your own pattern, you can purchase commercial mats designed for use in picture frames. Generally, these mats are available in a wide range of shapes and sizes. They are also made from heavy-duty cardboard, which holds up well when used as patterns. I have a variety of these mats in a range of shapes and sizes for use as patterns when making either mirrors or cabinets. Not only do these mats eliminate the need for making patterns, they also make a perfect outline of the shape and size needed. While somewhat expensive, they are well worth the investment.

Figure 3-43 presents a front view of the cabinet, along with its door and various dimensions. To assist in the placement of the hinges and also to present additional dimensions, Fig. 3-44 depicts a side view of the project.

Fig. 3-42. Small Cabinet with Door.

[1] Make the door for the cabinet from standard 1-×-10 material. Recall that a 10-inch standard board is actually 9¼ inches wide. As noted in Fig. 3-43, you will need to cut the door to a length of 12½ inches. Material of this width is rather expensive, so you might want to purchase only a minimum amount. Select the board carefully; often, wider stock can be bowed.

[2] Make the cabinet frame, shelf, and back boards from 1-×-4 stock.

Fig. 3-43. Front view of the Small Cabinet with Door.

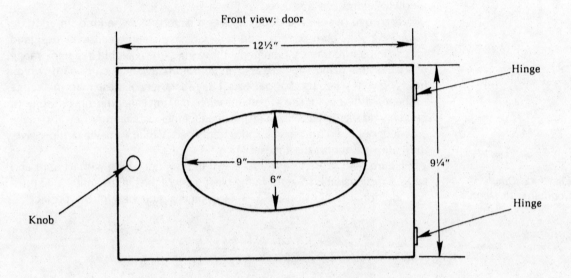

Front view: door

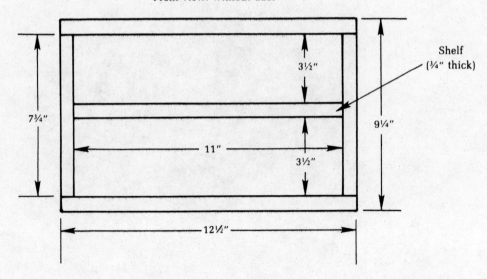

Front view: without door

Rip the back boards to a thickness of ¼ inch or less. An alternative is to use plywood for the back piece. Allowing for waste, you will need at least 6 feet of 1-×-4 material for the cabinet frame and shelf. If you plan to use ripped strips for the back section of the cabinet, you will need more material.

Measure and cut the various cabinet pieces using the dimensions provided in Fig. 3-43. Take your time when measuring and cutting the various parts. As you will note, the frame of the cabinet is 9¼ inches wide. It is critical that the two side pieces are cut to a length of exactly 7¾ inches. Accuracy is also necessary when cutting the shelf to length.

[3] You will need to make or purchase an oval pattern for preparing the area in the door that will accommodate the glass. The oval pattern should approximate the dimensions presented in Fig. 3-43. Of course, you might prefer to make the oval area smaller than the size suggested.

After centering the pattern on the door piece, trace the outline on the surface. Drill a ¼-inch-diameter hole inside the pattern area for placement of the saber saw blade. Very carefully, saw out the oval. Follow the pattern line so that the oval is as near perfect as you can make it.

Fig. 3-44. Side view of the Small Cabinet with Door.

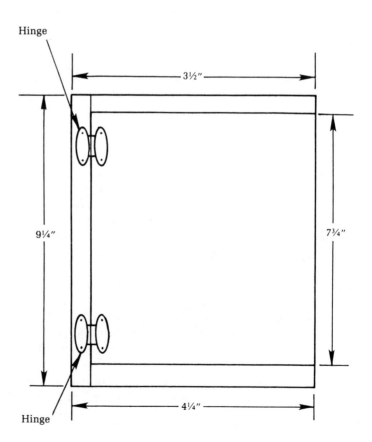

[4] Round-over the front edges of the door and the oval using a table-mounted router. Slightly round all other edges on the door and the cabinet with abrasive paper. I tend to do very little routing on this type of project.

Using a rabbeting router bit and a table-mounted router, rout a recess around the oval on the inside surface of the frame to accommodate the glass. The recess should be at least ⅛ inch deep. Refer to Project 7 for a discussion of this type of routing procedure. That project will also be helpful when you are ready to cut the glass.

[5] The inside back edges of the cabinet frame sections also need to be routed using a rabbeting bit. Rout a groove that is approximately ¼ inch or less deep in each piece. When the frame is assembled, these grooves will hold the back strips or plywood in place.

Rout the two side pieces with the rabbeting bit on their entire length. Rout the top and bottom pieces only to within ½ inch of their ends so the routed grooves do not show on the sides of the cabinet frame when it is assembled. You might want to think the routing procedure through before you actually make the cuts. Take your time with the rabbeting procedure and make several passes with the bit set at different depths.

[6] Sand all the surfaces to finishing readiness using a range of abrasive grits. It is much easier to sand the various parts before they are assembled. Be certain to lightly sand the nonrouted edges. Do not sand the edges that will be joined.

[7] Use the shelf as a guide when assembling the various parts. Using wood glue and finishing nails, assemble the cabinet frame. Be certain the routed grooves on the various parts are facing the inside of the frame. Refer to Fig. 3-45 prior to beginning the assembling procedures. To secure the shelf inside the cabinet frame, cut two pieces of 1- × -4-inch scrap material to a length of 4½ inches. Place these two pieces, with the cabinet standing upright, against the inside surfaces of the side pieces. Then place the shelf on top of these pieces for nailing. While the shelf is held in place on the scrap pieces, turn the cabinet on its side for nailing. The back edge of the shelf should be flush with the front edge of the grooves on the two side pieces to permit the back support boards to fit tightly against the back edge of the shelf.

While the shelf is resting on the two pieces of scrap, drive two finishing nails through the side piece and into the end of the shelf. Be certain to place the nails properly so that they will enter the center portion of the shelf. Repeat the process on the other end of the shelf.

The scrap pieces that are used for guides in the placement of the shelves can be any desired length. If you plan to place an item of a particular height on a shelf, measure and cut the scrap pieces accordingly. You can vary the distance between shelves and the two ends by making scrap guides of different lengths. Using guides is a very effective way of placing shelves in a cabinet. It also ensures that the shelves will be level when in place.

[8] Measure inside the routed grooves to determine the length of the boards or plywood needed for the back. Rip the boards to a thickness that will neatly fit inside the routed grooves. If plywood is to be used, purchase a thickness that will fit in the grooves. The ripped boards should be at least 1 inch wide and can run either up and down or lengthwise when in place.

Glue the pine strips or plywood and nail them in place using small headless brads. I usually stain or finish the cabinet before nailing the back board(s) in place. This makes the finishing process much easier.

[9] Measure and place the door knob as desired. You no doubt will need to drill a small-diameter hole through the door to receive the knob screw. Take your time with these procedures and be certain the knob is appropriately placed.

[10] Secure the hinges to the edge of the door and the side of the cabinet. You need to decide, even before the knob is secured, which side the door should open from. In most instances, this decision is based on where the finished shelf will be hung.

When securing the hinges, place the hinge knuckle directly over the space between the door and the frame. You might want to use clamps to hold the door against the frame while you are attaching the hinges. Place scraps between the clamps and the door surface so that the door is not marked or damaged. A yankee drill with small bits can be very useful for making pilot holes in the wood for the hinge screws. Take your time and think through the process when you are placing the hinges.

[11] After the hinges are in place, secure the door latch or magnetic catch on the door and inside the frame.

[12] You can obtain standard window glass from a local hardware store. As a rule, it is available in standard dimensions or it can be cut to your specifications. You might want to purchase enough for making two oval inserts. If you have never cut glass, use one piece for practice and learning.

For a detailed discussion on cutting glass, refer to Project 7. Be certain to add the width of the routed recess to the final dimensions of the glass.

Do not secure the glass in place until after the entire cabinet has been finished with whatever products you plan to use. A narrow bead of white glue spread around the recess will hold the glass in place.

PROJECT 16: LAMP

Given the cost of table lamps, you might want to consider making your own. This Lamp project (Fig. 3-45) affords you an opportunity to make a variety of lamps of different sizes for different rooms. Although I'm inclined to stain the lamps, you might want to consider painting them to blend more appropriately with a given room decor.

In addition to the fact that this project is relatively easy to make, the electrical components are readily available and simple to install. You will find that most hardware and discount stores sell lamp kits. These kits include everything you need for making the project into a functioning lamp. Best of all, the kits come with detailed instructions.

The sample project is of a size that requires a harp to hold the lamp shade.

Fig. 3-45. Lamp.

These harps, available in varying lengths, are also included in lamp kits. You need to obtain a kit with a harp length that is appropriate to the size of lamp.

It has been my experience that lamp and shade size are a matter of personal preference. There seem to be no guidelines as to what size lamp shade should be placed on what size lamp. It seems to be a matter of what looks best to the user. I have found that it is much easier to make the lamp than to decide on the appropriate size, color, and shape of the shade.

On smaller lamps, the harp component is not needed. Should you decide to make a small lamp, you can obtain shades that simply attach to the light bulb. You can easily modify or redesign this project into a smaller unit.

Figure 3-46 presents a side view of the project, as well as its various dimensions. This design requires a lamp kit with a harp and a shade that is dimensionally acceptable to the user. Figure 3-47 presents a top view of the lamp.

[1] The base of the lamp requires standard 1-×-10 stock. The base should be cut to a 9¼-inch square. (Recall that a 1-×-10 board is exactly 9¼ inches wide.) Refer to Figs. 3-46 and 3-47 as you measure and saw the parts. Measure and saw the base piece.

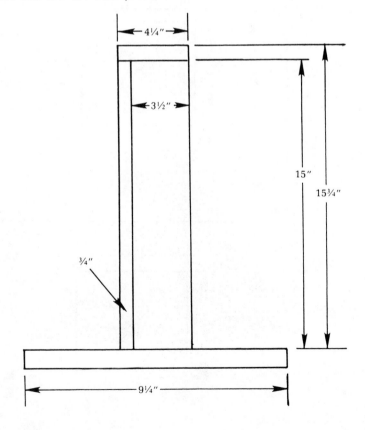

Fig. 3-46. Side view of the Lamp.

[2] The lamp post sides are made from 1-×-4 material. You will need at least 5½ feet of material for the four sides of the post. This length allows for some inevitable waste. Measure and cut the four sides of the post to a length of 15 inches.

[3] The top piece of the post requires a scrap of 1-×-6 or larger material. It needs to be a square piece that is 4¼ × 4¼ inches. Measure and saw the piece to these dimensions.

[4] Assemble the lamp post using wood glue and finishing nails. It is important that you refer to Fig. 3-47 to see how the sides of the post are assembled. The assembly method presented results in a lamp post that is exactly

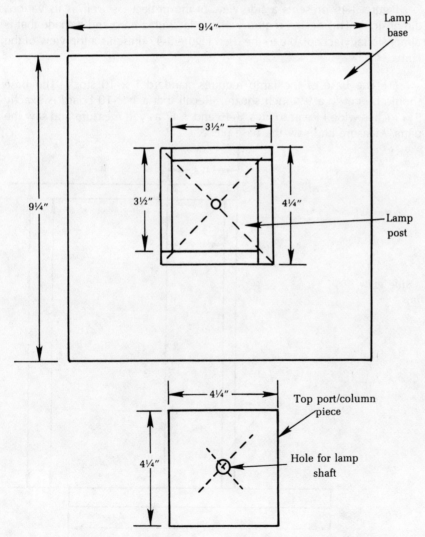

Fig. 3-47. Top view of the Lamp.

104

4¼ inches square. When assembling the pieces, be certain the ends of the boards are all flush with one another.

[5] Prior to beginning the next task, review the directions on the lamp kit that you plan to use for the project. Note that the kit contains a threaded brass nipple which screws into the bottom of the brass socket. The brass nipple, generally with an outside diameter of ⅜ inch, must penetrate the 4¼-inch-square piece that is attached to the top of the post. Mark the center of the top piece, and drill a hole that is small enough to hold the ⅜-inch nipple firmly in place. A ⁵⁄₁₆-inch-diameter bit or one that is even somewhat smaller is usually acceptable for making the hole. You might want to drill a practice hole in a scrap and test the nipple for fit.

[6] Spread wood glue on the top edges of the lamp post and place the 4¼-inch-square piece in place. Secure the piece to the post end using finishing nails. Wipe off any glue that squeezes onto the surfaces of the post.

[7] Do not rout the edges of the lamp post, including the top piece. Rout the top edges of the bottom piece using a round-over bit and a table-mounted router. Rout the edges on the bottom piece.

[8] In order for the electrical cord to penetrate through the bottom piece of the lamp, you must drill a hole at the exact center of the bottom piece. The hole should be at least ¾ inch in diameter.

A large hole through the bottom piece makes threading the electrical cord through it considerably easier. Thread the cord through the nipple held in the top piece of the post and down through the hole through the bottom piece. If a plug is secured to the electrical cord, you must reverse this procedure. In any event, a large hole makes the entire process easier. You will find that a long piece of wire, secured to the electrical cord, can greatly simplify this threading procedure. The lamp kit should provide some instructions for this procedure.

[9] You will need to rout a groove into the surface of the bottom piece to hold the electrical cord. The groove should extend from the drilled hole in the center to one of the edges. To simplify routing, rout the groove with the wood grain. For most electrical cords, a ¼-inch-wide-×-¼-inch-deep groove is adequate. You can force small wedges of wood into the groove to hold the cord in place.

[10] Sand all surfaces and edges using a range of abrasive grits. Lightly roll the edges of the lamp post and the top piece. Also bring the surfaces of the bottom piece to finishing readiness. Be certain you sand off any wood glue that might have dried on the surfaces.

[11] Prior to securing the lamp post to the bottom piece using wood glue and finishing nails, measure and mark its exact location on the bottom piece surface. I generally mark the outer edges of the post on both the top and bottom surfaces of the bottom piece. This procedure greatly simplifies and makes more accurate the nailing function. The post obviously needs to be centered on the bottom board.

Spread a bead of glue on the edges of the lamp post and place it on the bottom board's surface. Allow the glue to dry sufficiently so that the post is secure for the nailing procedure. Using finishing nails, nail the assembly together. You will want to use a nail punch to drive the heads of the nails below the surface to prevent the nails from scratching any surface upon which the lamp is placed.

[12] Follow the various procedures and instructions provided with the lamp kit. If you have never done any electrical work, the instructions are usually very basic and easy to follow.

PROJECT 17: SMALL WEED POTS

A project that is great fun on the lathe is the turning of weed pots (Fig. 3-48). The turning of small weed pots from scrap material is especially challenging. Although you might prefer to turn pots that are somewhat larger than the suggested project, you should at least try turning the smaller ones.

You can turn small weed pots with very simple lines or, if desired, you can embellish them with beads and other designs. As Fig. 3-48 suggests, I'm inclined to turn them with rather simple lines. Drill a small hole in the center top of the pot to hold a small weed or artificial flower. For small weed pots, a ⅛-inch-diameter hole is adequate.

Fig. 3-48. Small Weed Pots.

While I turn the small pots using spindle gouges, you can turn them using a ½-inch round scraper. This type of project provides you an opportunity to experiment with various turning tools. You can learn both what a tool can do and also its limitations. Turning small projects is an excellent way to develop your turning skills.

The project is spindle-turned using a four-prong drive center and a ball-bearing revolving center. Figure 3-49 presents a drawing of the lathe setup for turning the project. If available, you might want to use a miniature drive center instead of the larger four-prong drive. Also, if you do not have a ball-bearing revolving center, place a tailstock cup or dead center in the tailstock. It is best to rub some beeswax on the tailstock cup and point so they don't burn the wood during the turning process.

[1] The weed pots are best turned from pieces of either 2-×-4 or 2-×-6 material. Normally you will have scrap material of this thickness lying around the shop. Cut the spindle blanks into 1½-inch squares that are at least 2½ inches long. You might want to turn smaller pots but, generally, I turn them in lengths from 2½ to 4 inches. When sawing the spindle blanks, be certain the ends are square. Square ends will greatly simplify both mounting and turning of the blanks.

[2] Because pine is quite soft, you can easily drive the drive center into one end of the blank. Be certain the drive prongs are centered on the end of the spindle before you drive them into the wood. I use a large wooden mallet to drive the center into the wood. The other end of the spindle is resting

Fig. 3-49. Spindle for turning Weed Pots.

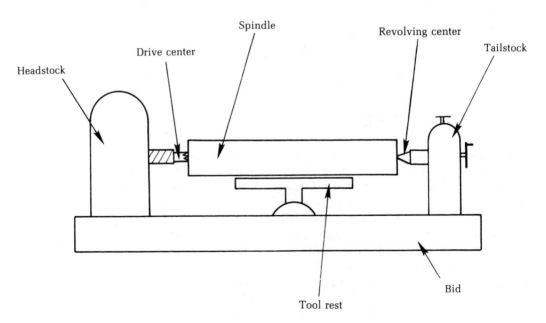

Headstock

Drive center

Spindle

Revolving center

Tailstock

Tool rest

Bid

107

on a concrete floor or other well-supported surface. The indentations made in the end of the wood will adequately keep the prongs in place once the assembly is mounted on the lathe.

On the other end of the spindle, make two diagonal lines from the corners. Where the two lines cross will be the center point. The revolving center or cup center point should penetrate at this mark.

With the drive center in the headstock, mount the spindle. Bring the tailstock forward with the revolving center or cup center penetrating the premarked center point. Secure the tailstock in place and align the tool rest for turning.

[3] True the spindle using either a roughing-out gouge or a ½-inch round-nose scraper. It is important that the square spindle initially be made round. Be careful that your turning tool does not make contact with the revolving drive center.

Using either a spindle gouge or a ½-inch round-nose scraper, shape the spindle as desired. Experiment with the tools and the wood. Try different cuts with the tools. As indicated earlier, this type of project is an excellent way to develop turning skills and knowledge of how various tools work on the wood. Turn the pot in a way and to a shape that is satisfying to you. Enjoy the process.

[4] If needed, sand the revolving piece using 100-grit abrasive paper. Follow with 150-grit and 220-grit paper. Bring the surface to a finishing readiness.

Although turned pieces can be finished while on the lathe, my own preference is to finish them off the lathe. You might want to try both methods and decide which one works best for you.

[5] Using the indentation made by the cup or revolving center, drill a ⅛- or ¼-inch-diameter hole into the pot. I generally drill the hole at least halfway through the pot. This depth makes the pot more able to hold weeds.

PROJECT 18: JAR COVERS

In recent years, turned lids for Mason-type jars have become very popular (Fig. 3-50). This project is somewhat more challenging than the previous turning project. The result, however, is a very attractive and functional jar lid or cover. As Fig. 3-50 suggests, you can turn the covers in a range of designs and use different types of knobs. In addition to some detailed turning, you can further embellish the covers by tole painting.

Once you understand the procedures involved in turning a jar cover, you can turn lids for jars other than the Mason type. As you will discover shortly, you must make a special screw chuck for turning the covers. Once the chuck is made, you can make covers of almost any diameter on it.

Figure 3-51 presents a cutaway of a standard jar cover, with some approximate dimensions. Although the top section of a Mason jar usually has an outside diameter of 2⅝ inches, you should definitely measure prior to turning. It is also important to note that you do not want the lid or cover to fit tightly over the top portion of the jar. I have found the dimensions presented in Fig. 3-51 to provide an effective fitting cover for standard Mason jars.

For turning the jar covers on the screw chuck, you will want to use scraping tools. In addition to a ½-inch round-nose scraper, you will need a ½-inch square-nose scraper for turning the inside area of the cover. Usually these two tools are adequate for turning the entire project.

The covers need to be turned from 2-inch-thick stock. It is best to use standard 2-×-6 material for the turning blocks. You can pattern them in a staggered fashion on the board to maximize the material. Hopefully you will have some scrap 2-×-6 material to use initially.

[1] As indicated, you must make a screw chuck for turning jar covers. Although any number of commercial screw chucks are available, it is quite a bit cheaper to make your own. They are just as effective and can be used for a range of other turning projects.

For making the screw chuck, you need a 3-inch faceplate, a 3½-inch round piece of hard maple, and a ¼-inch-diameter, 2½-inch-long lag screw. The hard maple should be 4/4s or 1 inch thick. Figure 3-52 presents a drawing of the screw chuck.

Center and mount the faceplate to the maple block. Be certain the faceplate screws do not penetrate through the front surface of the maple block. Thread the faceplate and block on the lathe and true the block using a round-nose scraper. Realign the tool rest so that it faces the front surface of the block. While the lathe is on, use the point of a skew chisel or similar tool to make

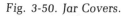

Fig. 3-50. Jar Covers.

an indentation at the center of the maple block. The revolving block will force the tool to the center. The indentation is the point where a hole will be drilled to receive the lag screw.

[2] Drill a hole that is approximately ³⁄₁₆ inch in diameter through the maple block at the point of the indentation. You need a hole that will allow the ¼-inch-diameter lag screw to penetrate the block, but one that is small enough to hold the screw firmly in place. Some faceplates have an open back that will permit a hole to be drilled through the block while mounted. On other faceplates, the block must be removed to drill the hole. If it is necessary to remove the block from the faceplate, make an alignment mark on the edge of the block and the faceplate. This will allow you to reattach the block to the faceplate without it being off center. You might need to drill a ¾-inch-diameter hole in the back surface of the block to accommodate the head of the lag screw.

[3] Thread the lag screw through the drilled hole in the block. You will need a socket wrench or similar tool to screw the lag through the hard maple. The head of the lag screw should be tight against the back surface of the block. If you had to remove the faceplate for this procedure, reattach it to the block using the alignment marks.

[4] Secure the chuck on the lathe and turn on the motor. Examine the end of the lag screw as it revolves. If it is not running true, turn off the lathe and tap the screw with a block of wood. You want the lag screw to run relatively true. Repeat the procedure until the lag runs true.

[5] Using a hacksaw, cut off the lag screw so that only 1 inch of it extends from the front surface of the maple block. With a small file, deepen the gullets between the threads on the lag. This procedure will give the lag screw better

Fig. 3-51. Cut-away of Jar Covers.

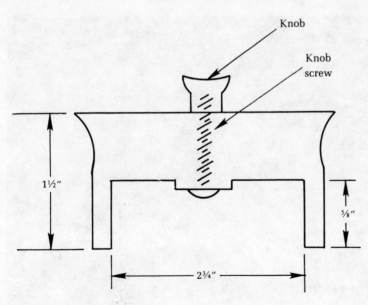

Knob

Knob screw

1½"

⅝"

2¾"

holding power on blocks. The screw chuck should now be ready to use.

[6] The cover or lid blocks are best cut from 2-×-6 material. Using a school compass set for a diameter of 3⅝ inches, make a circle on the wood's surface. Use a pencil to mark the small indentation made by the point of the compass. This will give you the exact center of the block and the point at which a ³⁄₁₆-inch-diameter or smaller hole needs to be drilled. Cut out the block using either a band or saber saw. I would suggest you prepare more than one block while doing these initial procedures. It is almost impossible to only turn one item on the lathe and then quit.

[7] After the blocks have been cut, drill the small pilot holes through the centers. The holes need to be large enough to thread on the lag screw, but small enough to firmly grip the screw.

[8] With the screw chuck on the lathe, thread a block on the lag screw. Make sure the block is tight against the front surface of the chuck. Align the tool rest on the side of the block just above its midpoint. Using a ½-inch round-nose scraper, true the block and leave the wall straight. Don't remove any more wood than is necessary to bring the block to perfect roundness.

[9] Realign the tool rest to the front of the block again, just above its

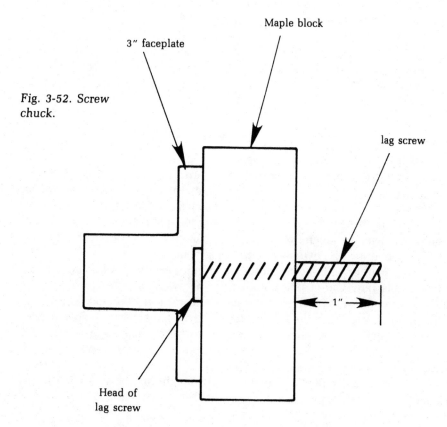

Fig. 3-52. Screw chuck.

3″ faceplate

Maple block

lag screw

1″

Head of lag screw

midpoint. The next procedure involves removing wood from the block for that part of the cover that fits over the jar. Refer to Fig. 3-51 to note how the area will look and also its dimensions. The dimensions given are for a standard-diameter Mason jar. If your cover is for another type of jar, determine its diameter prior to turning out the cover area.

A ½-inch square-nose scraper is the ideal tool for removing wood from this area of the cover. Note in Fig. 3-51 how a small tenon is left in the center of this area. This tenon is for the screw that holds the lid knob in place. The length of the tenon is determined by the length of the screw used for a particular knob. You might want to check the screw length on the knob you will be using. Turn out the area to the required dimensions.

[10] Before removing the block to turn the top surface of the cover, sand the side and the bottom edge of the cover. You also might want to lightly sand inside the turned area.

[11] Remove the block from the lag screw, reverse it, and rethread it on the lag. This procedure will enable you to turn the top surface of the cover. Prior to doing any turning on the top surface, you might want to refer to Fig. 3-50 to get a few ideas. After deciding how you want the surface turned, use a ½-inch round-nose scraper to achieve it. When turning is completed, sand the entire surface using a range of abrasive grits. Bring the surfaces to finishing readiness.

[12] The final procedure is to secure the knob to the top of the cover. In most instances, the knob screw will fit through the predrilled pilot hole that was used for turning. If it is too small, redrill it with a wider bit. Secure the knob to the cover and finish.

PROJECT 19: SMALL BOWL

The lathe is the ideal tool for making bowls, regardless of size. In many ways, pine is an excellent wood from which to turn bowls (Fig. 3-53). Although bowls are more often considered functional, they can be very decorative. The grain and other natural characteristics of pine make for an extremely attractive piece. If you are so inclined, you can paint or tole-paint pine bowls to further enhance them. Although many turners disparage the use of pine for bowls, I have found it to be extremely challenging and satisfying.

The Small Bowl project is designed to introduce you to the procedures for turning bowls from pine. Unlike the hardwoods, pine is not readily available in thickness that exceed 2 inches. Thus, it is necessary to glue up boards to achieve the desired thickness. While the project employs two pieces of 2-×-6 stock, you can glue together standard 1-inch material to achieve the desired thickness. An interesting effect for a bowl is to glue pieces of veneer between 1-inch-thick pine boards. This type of laminating process results in some very attractive pieces. To increase the height of a bowl, simply laminate more boards together.

You can achieve different effects by reversing the boards so that their grain runs in opposite directions. This is especially effective if you use 1-×-10 boards for the laminating procedure. These larger boards enable you to turn a much wider bowl that exposes more wood surface. The same effect can be achieved by using wider 2-inch-thick stock.

Before beginning the project, you might want to do some planning and design work. You also might prefer to prepare and turn something a bit larger or more decorative. Much of the fun in wood turning is the preparation of the turning blocks, especially when you are laminating boards together.

The project bowl is turned using a 3-inch faceplate. You can use either scrapers or bowl gouges for the actual turning process. If you are new at the lathe, you might want to use scraping tools initially. You will find them to be extremely effective on pine. Also, you will be assured of a more successful and enjoyable experience on the lathe.

[1] For turning the project bowl, you will need at least 12 inches of 2-×-6 stock. These dimensions should result in a bowl that has a diameter of about 4¾ inches and is 3 inches high. Using a school compass, make two circles with a 5½-inch diameter on the surface of the stock. Mark the compass point indentation with a pencil so it can be easily seen. This mark will assist you in centering the faceplate on the block.

Cut out the two round blocks using either a band saw or a saber saw. Take your time while sawing so you have reasonably round blocks. It makes the turning process somewhat easier and also minimizes wood waste.

[2] Spread a light coating of wood glue on one surface of each block. The glue should be spread over the entire surface of both blocks. Don't spread glue on the surfaces where you have the center marked with a pencil. Join the blocks together and clamp using several bar or C clamps. The blocks often slide on the glue during the clamping procedure. If this happens, realign

Fig. 3-53. Small Bowl.

the blocks and reclamp. You want the edges of the blocks to be flush. Allow the assembly to dry adequately before you remove the clamps.

[3] Using the center pencil mark as a guide, mount a 3-inch faceplate to the joined block. Because pine is quite soft, you should use screws that will penetrate at least ⅝ inch into the base of the block. Shorter screws might not hold the block in place during the turning process. Be certain the faceplate is centered on the block.

[4] Thread the faceplate and the block onto the lathe. Align the tool rest at the side of the block, just above its midpoint. You must true and shape the side of the block before you can remove wood from the inside. For truing and shaping the block, use either a ½- or 1-inch round-nose scraper. Don't apply too much pressure with the tool because you could force the block from the faceplate screws. After you have trued the block, shape the side of the bowl as desired. (Refer to Fig. 3-53.)

[5] When the side has been shaped as desired, align the tool rest in front of the block. Again, the tool rest should be just above the midpoint of the bowl. As you know, scrapers should be used by pointing the front end slightly downward into the wood. This procedure can be done effectively only if the tool rest is above the midpoint of the block.

The inside area of the block is best turned using a ½-inch round-nose scraper. Turn the inside of the bowl, leaving the upper portion of the wall at least ⅛ inch thick. If the wall is turned too thin, it is more likely to chip or break. When you are turning out the bottom portion of the inside, remember the faceplate screws that are penetrating into the block. You might want to leave the bottom area relatively thick.

[6] Sand the inside and outside surfaces of the bowl starting with 100-grit abrasive paper. Lightly roll the top edge of the bowl. Finish sanding the bowl using 150- and 220-grit abrasive paper. If the end-grain areas remain rough, stop the lathe and work on them with the abrasives. Pine has rather coarse end grain and it is often difficult to get smooth.

[7] Remove the faceplate from the finished bowl. Place wood filler in the screw holes in the bottom of the bowl. When the filler is dry, sand the bottom surface with a belt or palm sander.

PROJECT 20: WOODEN SPOON

In addition to those methods already presented, other ways to make small pine projects such as a Wooden Spoon (Fig. 3-54), are by carving or whittling. Although the two methods are somewhat different approaches to working with wood, most people use the terms interchangeably. It is not our concern to define terms, but rather to learn how to make projects from pine. At some point, you might want to explore the literature that is available on these subjects. As you will discover, carving or whittling are both fascinating and thoroughly enjoyable methods of working with wood.

There is an array of tools available for carving or whittling projects from pine or any other wood. Figure 3-55 presents some of the various tools that I use when making pine projects. In addition to the carving tools and knives, the photograph includes a scorp. While by no means a mandatory tool, the small scorp can be very useful in making wooden spoons. It is a roughing-out tool that can be used to remove wood quickly from the *bill* or front portion, of a spoon. I find it especially useful when carving a spoon with a rather deep bill area.

If you are inclined to using carving or whittling tools which are very popular with woodcarvers, Fig. 3-56 presents a commonly used set. This type of set has a range of interchangeable knives that can make almost any type of cut. Lest we forget, there is also the standard jackknife, which is used by many lay and professional carvers. Probably, most whittling is still done using a common, readily available jackknife. You might want to consider using one for the presented projects.

It has been my experience that more important than the type of tool used is the ability to sharpen a blade or edge. Knives or tools that are to be used for carving or whittling must be extremely sharp. Dull tools present the greatest hazard to the would-be carver. You would be well advised to practice and develop some skill in sharpening your various tools. A number of books listed in the Bibliography will provide some information on this critical task.

In recent years, carvers also have been using a wide variety of small, hand electric tools. In addition to the various flexible-shaft tools that are available, the small Dremel tool is an excellent unit to assist you in making pine projects. There is a wide range of burrs, mandrels, and sanding sleeves that are available for Dremel tools. Various devices, including a Dremel tool, are presented in Chapter 2. The sanding sleeves are available in a range of abrasive grits and are excellent for both shaping and finishing small projects. Power tools greatly simplify the carving process. You might want to consider purchasing one of these tools to assist you in your carving activities.

Another tool that I use in carving small projects is a small, electric pad sander. It is often called a *finishing sander*. This type of tool is excellent for both shaping and finishing projects. A 60- or 80-grit abrasive secured to the tool can shape a piece of pine into a project very quickly. The use of this type of tool can eliminate a great deal of wood removal normally done with a knife. It is not quite as romantic, but it is certainly more efficient.

As you will note in the discussion on carving spoons, it is best to pattern a project on a board and then rough-cut it using a band or saber saw. This eliminates a great deal of unnecessary work with a knife. Most carvers pattern and cut their carving blanks to shape using some type of saw. This procedure produces a project that is more accurate dimensionally, and also saves a great deal of work.

While basswood is generally preferred by carvers, you will find that pine is an excellent carving wood. On occasion, you might need to work around

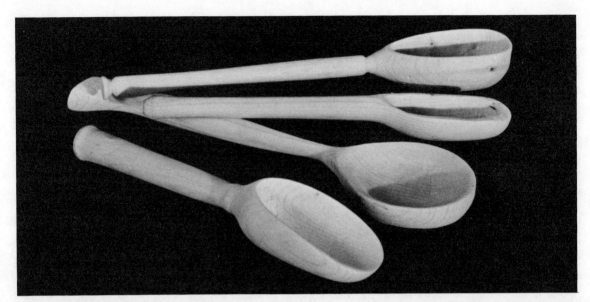

Fig. 3-54. Wooden Spoons.

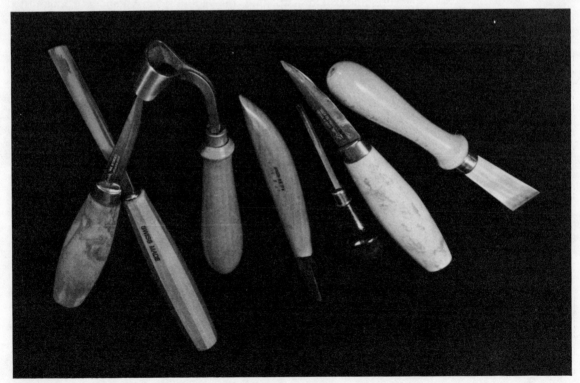

Fig. 3-55. Carving tools, knives and scorp.

a knot. I often pattern a project on a board, avoiding inclusion of knots from any critical part of a piece. With some projects, you will want to include an attractive knot or two. Unlike basswood, pine tends to come off in long slivers when it is carved. Take your time when using a knife and make your cuts short and deliberate. You might need to make extra cuts into the wood's surface to avoid splintering.

As with any tool, use common sense when you are working with carving tools and knives. To be effective and safe, carving tools and knives, must be exceptionally sharp. This also means that, when misused, they can quickly cut flesh. You might want to wear a leather glove to hold the piece being carved. A glove often will prevent some of the minor cuts that can occur. Plan your cuts and anticipate the direction of the tool's edge or point.

Wooden spoons, as you are no doubt aware, can be made in an array of sizes and shapes. You can carve spoons that will have a specific function, i.e. serving spoons and small scoops. Many wooden spoons, often called *treenware*, can be used for decorative purposes only. Holes can be drilled in the handles for holding a strand of leather for hanging. If you are inclined to doing tole, spoons lend themselves to being painted with designs. Once you have carved your first spoon, you will find yourself fascinated with the possibilities for both design and function.

Fig. 3-56. Carving knives (courtesy of Warren Tool Co., Inc.).

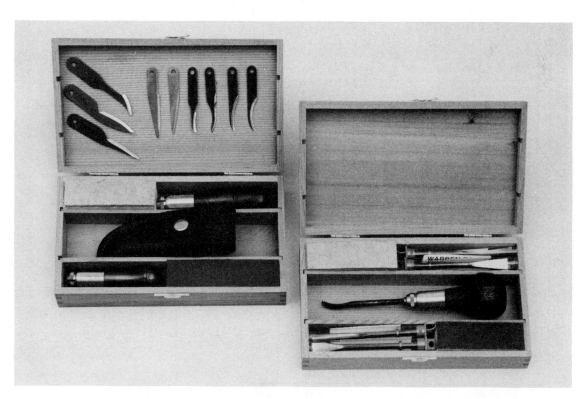

The collection of spoons in Fig. 3-54 were carved from either standard 1- or 2-inch-thick pine. You will find that scrap pieces of pine can be readily used for carving spoons and some of the later carving projects. Wooden spoons do not need to be large. Small sugar spoons or demitasse spoons are great fun to carve. Their small size makes them especially challenging. Do some design and planning work prior to initiating your projects. If you need to buy tools, you may want to refer to the mail-order suppliers listed in the Appendix.

[1] Determine both the length and thickness of the spoon design you plan to carve. These dimensions will determine whether you should use 1- or 2-inch-thick stock. Remember that 1-inch standard pine is only ¾-inch thick and 2-inch is 1½ inches thick.

Draw the spoon design of both the bill and the handle on the board. Draw the pattern oversize and following the grain of wood because the spoon needs to be rounded by carving away wood. Figure 3-57 depicts a pattern drawn onto the surface of the board.

[2] Using a band saw or saber saw, cut the spoon blank from the board. If you are using a band saw, you can remove additional wood from the bottom portion of the handle. Leave the bill its full thickness. As a rule, I remove as much excess wood as possible with a band saw. This process greatly reduces

Fig. 3-57. Wood Spoon pattern.

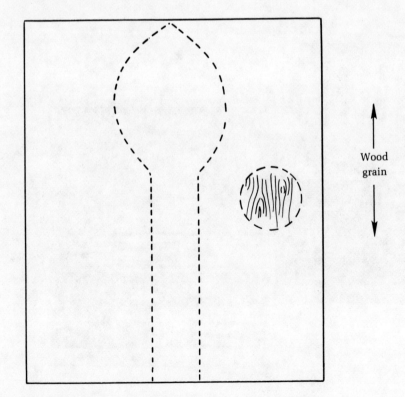

Wood grain

118

the amount of time and energy needed for the actual carving of the piece.

[3] As suggested, there are any number of small electric tools you can use to do the initial shaping of the spoon. For an initial carving project, you might want to use a carving knife or a jackknife.

Begin with the knife by shaping the handle round. Don't remove too much wood at first. Next, shape the spoon bill to roughly conform with your design. If you plan to have a deep bill that will hold liquids or other items, don't remove too much of the wood's thickness. Incidentally, the handle of the spoon should connect with the top portion of the bill. Keep this in mind as you do the initial shaping.

[4] For removing wood from the inside area of the bill, a small scorp is the ideal tool. Another effective carving tool is a spoon gouge. If you do not have any of these tools, you can drill wood out of the bill area, then use Forstner bits or brad point bits to remove excess wood from the bill. If you use this procedure, be careful not to drill too deeply. The point of the bit could penetrate through the bottom surface. If the width of your spoon design is very narrow, drilling the wood out might be the best option. During any of these procedures, keep the wall a uniform thickness.

You can clean up the inside area of the bill easily by using a Dremel tool with sanding sleeves, or you can do it by hand using 60- or 80-grit abrasive paper. It is important to keep the wall a uniform thickness.

[5] If you are having difficulty removing the wood from the bill area, you can always make the spoon into a scoop. Refer to Fig. 3-54 and note the front portion of the pictured scoop. It is essentially a deep spoon with the front portion of the bill wall removed.

Using a band or saber saw, cut the front portion of the bill at a slight angle. You can remove the wood inside the bill with a knife or any number of other tools.

[6] After the wood has been removed from the handle and bill area, sand the surface using a range of abrasives. As indicated, start with a coarse grit for quick wood removal and shaping. Be certain to sand with the wood grain. Keep sanding the surface with increasingly finer grits until you have brought the spoon to finishing readiness. If you prefer, drill a small hole through the handle for hanging the spoon.

If the spoon is to be used with food items, be certain you finish it with one of the nontoxic products that are available.

PROJECT 21: PIG CUTTING BOARD

While the Pig Cutting Board (Fig. 3-58) will last longer if made from hard maple, pine is adequate and will provide many years of service. Many colonial cutting boards were, in fact, made from pine. In addition to serving as a very functional piece, this project also can be hung for decoration. This project presents considerable surface for tole painting.

The pattern for this project is one that has been in my family for many years. It seems that most families have some type of pig cutting board that's been around for years. I initially traced this design from a very worn pine cutting board used by my mother. It seems that her board was traced from one used by her mother. As with many of these kinds of designs and objects, to isolate their point of origin is almost impossible. In any event, I have found it to be a very attractive and functional design that is relatively easy to cut.

The size of the cutting board can be varied based on available material and your own needs and tastes. I generally make a large pig that is approximately 8½ inches wide and 16 inches long. This size can be easily cut from a 1-×-10 pine board. For decorative hanging pigs and cheese boards, I also made smaller ones in a variety of sizes. You might want to modify the suggested measurements and make a board that meets your particular needs.

To assist you in preparing a pattern for the project, Fig. 3-59 presents an outline of the project, along with some dimensions. Space does not permit the outline to be dimensionally accurate, but it should assist you in drawing the pattern needed.

[1] Measure and cut a piece of 1-×-10 stock to a length of 17 inches. While the actual length of the project is 16 inches, you will need the extra length for patterning and cutting.

[2] Prepare a pattern using the outline and dimensions provided in Fig. 3-59. It is important to remember that the pig outline or pattern doesn't need

Fig. 3-58. Pig Cutting Board.

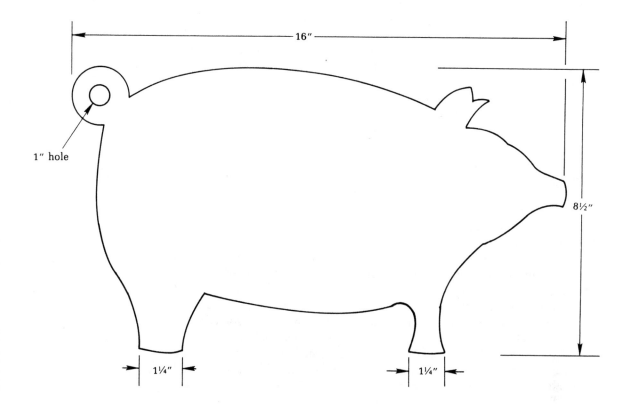

16"

1" hole

8½"

1¼"   1¼"

Fig. 3-59. Dimensions for Pig Cutting Board.

to be perfect. The design only approximates a pig. Modify the pattern according to your tastes and ideas on how a pig should look. Trace the pattern on the 17-inch-long 1-×-10 board and cut out the pig using a saber saw.

[3] Drill a 1-inch-diameter hole in the tail area. This hole not only makes the design more attractive, but is also used for hanging. Rout the edges on both sides of the pig using a round-over bit mounted on a router table. Also, rout the drilled tail hole. You might prefer to use abrasive paper for rounding the edges.

[4] Using a range of abrasive grits, sand the surfaces and edges of the pig to finishing readiness.

PROJECT 22: FISH

This project is a wall plaque that has carved details on its surface (Fig. 3-60). It represents one of many possibilities for combining a sawed design with carved surface details. A similar plaque can be done of a cat, birds, flowers, landscapes, or any number of other objects or scenes. The fish design was somewhat challenging because I had to figure out how to do the scales.

For doing surface details on this type of project, you need to use a number of standard carving tools. There are any number of small, palm-handled carving sets on the market that are excellent for this kind of carving. These smaller tools are generally about 4½ to 5 inches long, and the sets contain most of the basic tools needed. Figure 3-61 pictures a set that I have found very useful. You can cut with these tools very easily by forcing them with the palm of your hand. You will need to keep the tools very sharp by using a variety of appropriate stones.

To limit your investment in carving tools, you can use one or two larger carving tools to do most detail work on plaques. Professional carving tools are usually about 9 to 12 inches long. A narrow, deep gouge or a small veiner gouge are effective for doing surface detail. You can make cuts into the wood's surface easily with palm pressure only. Pine is very soft so a carver's mallet is not needed.

You will find that a number of the mail-order suppliers listed in the Appendix maintain a complete inventory of carving tools and related supplies. The catalogs can be extremely informative in terms of understanding what the various tools can do to wood.

In addition to the range of carving tools that are available, you can also improvise with other devices to achieve a particular surface effect. For example, to make the scales on the fish, I used a standard steel punch. The tip of the punch was ⅛ inch in diameter. Using a standard hammer, I tapped the punch to make the rows of scales on the surface. The scales not only look

Fig. 3-60. Carved Fish.

real, but also feel real. The edges raised by the punch are somewhat rough, giving the surface a very scaley feel. Don't limit yourself to standard carving tools if you want to achieve a particular effect. Experiment on the wood with a range of devices.

You can vary the dimensions for the fish project easily. I generally make it approximately 8 inches long and 4¾ inches wide. It is easily cut from a standard piece of 1-×-6 material.

[1] To make the project design, you will need a piece of 1-×-6 stock that is at least 9 inches long. This will provide ample length for the project with a bit to spare.

[2] Although the fish design can be drawn freehand onto the board's surface, you might want to make a pattern. The tail area offers some opportunity to experiment with the shape. Pattern the design onto the board's surface and cut it out using a saber saw.

Fig. 3-61. Palm carving tools (courtesy of Warren Tool Co., Inc.).

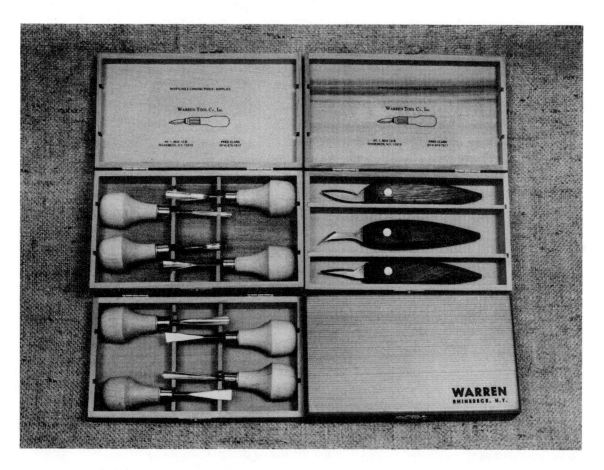

[3] To simplify and ensure greater accuracy when carving the details, pencil the various parts of the fish onto the board's surface. I pencil the details in exactly to the length and width that I want to carve. Although you can carve the details without this procedure, it is more difficult and the result is less attractive. Take your time in drawing the details until they are exactly the way you want the finished piece to appear.

[4] Generally, you should make cuts with the tool beginning on the inside and moving to the outer edge. This procedure will give a narrow and shallow entry cut and a wide, deep exit cut. Practice carving on a piece of scrap. When you feel somewhat confident about making the cut, proceed with the project. Try to make the cuts with but one movement of the tool. Carve all the details as penciled.

[5] Using a steel punch and hammer, make small scales on the surface. They should be punched in rows to approximate the appearance of scales. Keep the depth of the punches reasonably uniform.

[6] Slightly roll the edges of the fish using abrasive paper. You might want to sand the carved surface using a fine-grit abrasive. Secure a small picture hanger to the center back of the plaque for hanging.

PROJECT 23: BIRD ON STAND

Carving small birds for placement on a dowel and block are both fun and very challenging projects (Fig. 3-62). While I'm inclined to carve only the rounded outline of a bird, you might want to experiment with more detail. Most bird identification books provide a series of excellent silhouettes of common song birds. Similar books are available that provide both the silhouette and details of a range of shore birds.

As you would guess, birds can be carved in a range of sizes. The project bird is approximately 5½ inches long and 1½ inches wide. It was carved from a chunk of 2-×-4 stock. The bird is supported by a 4-inch-long piece of ¼-inch-diameter dowel that is secured in a piece of firewood. For making larger birds, glue and clamp either 2-×-4 stock or 2-×-6 material. If you spread wood glue over both surfaces and clamp the assembly properly, the block will hold together indefinitely. Be certain to allow the glue to dry properly. This is an excellent way to make carving blocks for large birds or other carving projects.

It is best to make a pattern of the project and then trace it on the wood to be used (Fig. 3-63). Be certain to place the pattern and trace it with the wood grain.

[1] After designing the type, shape, and size of bird you want to carve, make a pattern using construction paper. Trace the pattern on the surface of a piece of 2-×-4 stock. Hopefully, you will have some pieces of scrap material around to use for an initial project. Cut out the traced design using ei-

ther a band or saber saw. If you use a band saw, you can remove additional wood from the edges of the blank. To simplify the carving process, you want to remove as much wood as you can with the saw.

[2] I prefer using a carving knife with this project. It can, of course, be done with a jackknife. Using the knife, bring the bird to shape. You will find the tail and beak areas are often the most difficult. Keep in mind that you are only carving a silhouette of a bird. The carving will only approximate the outline of a bird. You might want to do more detailed work later using either

Fig. 3-62. Bird on Stand.

Fig. 3-63. Pattern for Bird on Stand.

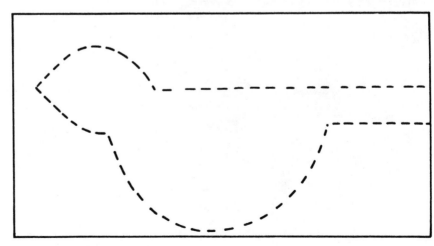

carving tools or a woodburning unit.

You can also do shaping using a wood rasp or a Dremel tool with sanding sleeves. Use a coarse-grit abrasive for shaping. You will find the Dremel or a flex-shaft tool to be excellent for shaping bird projects. You might want to consider using one of the numerous carbide burrs that are available for these tools.

[3] After the bird has been carved and shaped to its final form, go over its entire surface with a range of abrasive grits, either by hand or with a small electric finishing sander. Prepare the surface for the finishing process.

[4] If a dowel is to be used to support the bird, drill a hole in the bottom center. Cut a piece of ¼-inch-diameter dowel to the desired length. If the dowel is too long, the bird tends to tip over.

[5] Using either a piece of pine or a chunk of firewood, cut a base piece that is large enough to hold the bird. Drill a ¼-inch-diameter hole in its center to receive the dowel. Finish as desired.

PROJECT 24: TWO BIRDS ON A WOOD BLOCK

While another bird carving project, Two Birds on a Wood Block (Fig. 3-64) is somewhat different from the previous design. This one involves two rather small birds with wire legs secured to a piece of log. It is an enjoyable project to make and is a rather attractive decorative piece when finished. As in the previous project, the birds are carved silhouettes. You can, if desired, give them some feather, eye, and beak detail using either small carving tools or a woodburning unit. The birds also can be painted.

The birds for the project can be carved from 2-inch-thick stock. I usually make them approximately 4 inches long and about 1¼ inches wide. I attempt to make each bird somewhat different from the other both in size and shape. They can be stained to make them appear like different birds.

Fig. 3-64. Two Birds on a Wood Block.

The base that the birds are secured to is a slice of a 5-inch-diameter log. I chop the slice in half using a hatchet. This tends to give the block a more rustic appearance than if it were sawed. The bark should be left on the log. I usually cut the log slice to a thickness of about 1½ inches, which is more than adequate to support the birds. The base greatly enhances the overall project. I have also carved small mushrooms and secured them to the top surface of the base. Other items also could be carved and secured to the base surface. Use your imagination.

To secure the birds to the base, legs can be made from ¹⁄₁₆-inch-diameter wire. The wire can be easily bent to approximate legs. Figure 3-65 shows how the leg wires are bent and inserted into the birds and the block. The ends of the wires are glued as they are inserted in place.

[1] Make a pattern of both birds from construction paper. Trace the patterns on the surface of 2-inch stock and cut out the carving blank. Refer to Project 23 for a discussion on various carving procedures and tools that are helpful in making the birds. Using a range of abrasive grits, prepare the birds for finishing.

[2] Using a band saw or a long blade on a saber saw, cut a slice of log approximately 1½ inches thick, and at least 5 inches in diameter. Split the log slice into two pieces using either an axe or hatchet. If neither is available, split the log with a hammer and wood chisel. Leave any firmly attached bark in place to enhance the project. Sand the top surface of the log slice to finishing readiness.

Fig. 3-65. Wire bird legs.

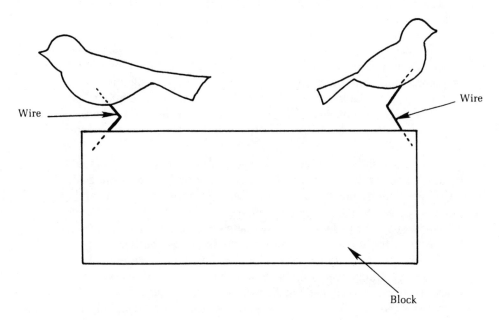

Wire

Wire

Block

[3] Legs need to be prepared for each of the birds. Use wire that is approximately 1/16 inch in diameter. Cut four strands of wire approximately 1¼ inches long. Figure 3-65 shows how to bend the wires to approximate the legs. You can bend the wires to shape easily using a standard pliers.

[4] Using a 1/16-inch-diameter bit, drill two holes in the center bottom of each bird. They should be about 1/8 inch apart and should be at least 3/8 inch deep. Drill the holes at a slight angle toward the front of the bird.

[5] Plan where the birds should be placed on the top surface of the log. You need to allow sufficient room for each as you plan where to drill the wire holes. Mark the two points where wire holes should be drilled for each bird. They should be about 1/8 inch apart. Drill the wire holes for both birds.

[6] Spread white glue on the ends of the wires and insert them into the bottom of the birds. Next, spread glue on the other ends and insert the wires into the base piece. Before the glue dries, adjust the birds on their wires to their final positions. Allow the glue to dry.

[7] The method you use to finish the birds should determine when you should glue them in place. They can be easily stained and/or lacquered while secured to the base. If you plan to paint the birds or give them some other kind of detailed finish, these procedures should be done prior to securing them to the leg wires.

PROJECT 25: HANGING NECKLACE HOLDER

If you need a hanging holder for necklaces, this design is a good option (Fig. 3-66). In that it is a hanging piece, you might prefer a scroll plaque design as opposed to a straight piece of wood. If you wish to tole-paint the project, you might want a design that will accommodate a particular pattern.

The project can be designed to dimensions that will permit placement of the holder in a particular location. While Fig. 3-67 presents the sample project along with dimensions, you might want to modify it significantly to be placed in a particular location in a room. The project is made from standard 1-×-4 stock, but you might prefer a wider holder made from 1-×-6 lumber. Again, do some design work so that the project will meet your special needs.

[1] Measure and cut a piece of 1-×-4 lumber to a length of at least 10 inches. You might want to cut it a bit longer to make both patterning and sawing easier. This eliminates the need to work from the actual ends of the board. As suggested in other projects, I often cut the boards an extra ½ inch long to allow space for patterns and saw-blade entry. This procedure wastes a little material, but it makes the various tasks somewhat easier.

[2] Although the pattern presented in Fig. 3-67 can be done freehand on the board, you might want to prepare a pattern from construction paper. The pattern will assist you in making the two sides of the holder exactly alike. If you plan for more elaborate scrollwork in the project, you definitely will

want to prepare a pattern. Cut the board to the desired design using a saber saw.

[3] Measure and mark the location of the ¼ inch diameter dowels on the board's surface. As Fig. 3-67 indicates, the sample project employs seven dowels placed in the board. The distance between the dowels should be equal so the holder has a balanced appearance. You might prefer to use more dowels. In part, the number of dowels used should be determined by how many items you plan to hang on the holder.

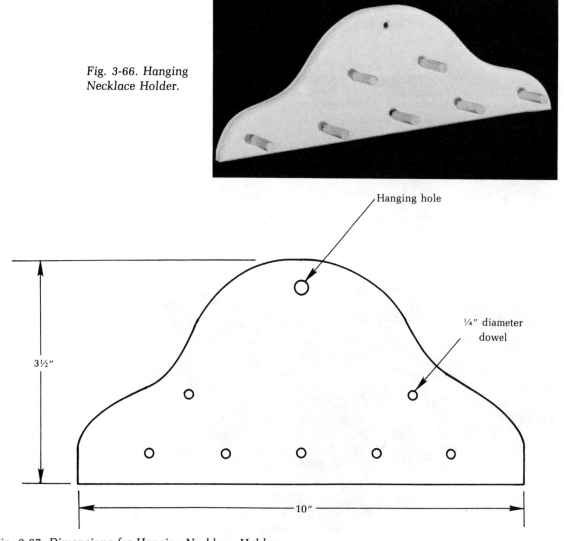

Fig. 3-66. Hanging Necklace Holder.

Fig. 3-67. Dimensions for Hanging Necklace Holder.

Also mark the hanging hole. Be certain that you measure and place this hole in the exact center of the board. Use a ¼-inch-diameter drill bit to make the hanging hole and also the dowel holes. Drill all of the dowel holes to an equal depth.

[4] You can either rout the edges of the board using a table-mounted router and a round-over bit, or you can sand it. You definitely want to roll the edges slightly. This greatly enhances the appearance of the holder. Also, sand the surfaces to finishing readiness.

[5] Round-over the ends of the dowels slightly using abrasive paper.

[6] Using either a toothpick or wood splinter, spread wood glue on the walls of the dowel holes. Tap the dowels into their holes and wipe off any glue that is forced onto the board's surface. Be certain you tap the dowels to the bottom of their holes.

PROJECT 26: SCONCES

With the candle holders and reflective mirrors, this project is clearly decorative (Fig. 3-68). While you might prefer to make only a single sconce, traditionally they are displayed in pairs. Thus, as you plan for the project, you should probably think in terms of making a pair of sconces.

Fig. 3-68. Sconces.

The candle holders that are attached to the back pieces have drilled holes in them to accommodate the candle bases; however, you might prefer to use commercial candle cups that are available from various mail-order suppliers. A number of these suppliers are listed in the Appendix. I prefer having the drilled holes because the candle cups seem too conspicuous on this design. They tend to overwhelm the sconces. Your own design work and tastes might, however, suggest their use. If you plan to use commercial candle cups, you might want to make the sconce back piece both longer and wider to give the entire project a more balanced appearance.

Another factor to consider in your design activities is whether or not you want to light candles occasionally. It seems that most sconces display the candles solely for appearance and not for use. If you plan to light the candles, the holder piece should be long to keep the flame away from the back piece and the mirror. In part, this decision is affected by both the length and diameter of the candles to be used. The project design is of a size where the candles could be lit, if desired; however, you should monitor the sconces while the candles are burning.

As suggested, you can easily increase the length and width of the project if desired. You might have a location where you prefer to have larger sconces. You can use the same basic design even though the dimensions are different. Figure 3-69 presents the project, as well as various dimensions.

[1] The project is best made from 1-×-6 material. While you will have some waste, this width board will minimize it. To simplify both the patterning and sawing functions, cut two boards to a length of 13 inches each. This will provide ample length for a pair of sconces. You can easily make the candle holder pieces from scraps.

[2] You will want to make a pattern for both the back piece and the candle holder. Use the folded construction paper method described in other projects. It is the easiest way to make a pattern where both sides of the design will be exactly the same. Use this same patterning method for the candle holders. Refer to Fig. 3-69 for the various dimensions.

[3] You should also make a pattern for the cut-out mirror area in the center of the sconces. You can again use the folded-paper method. Use the dimensions presented in Fig. 3-69 when making the pattern. Also, note the appearance of the mirror areas, as pictured in Fig. 3-68. You might prefer to modify the shape of the mirror area to something more to your liking. The mirror area pattern will also be of use when cutting the actual mirror glass. More about this shortly.

Prepare the necessary patterns for the project.

[4] Trace the pattern for the back piece on both pieces of 13-inch-long stock that you cut earlier. Using a saber saw, carefully saw out the back pieces. Cut along the pattern lines so that the sconces look exactly alike. Take your time with this sawing function.

[5] Center the mirror area pattern on the back pieces and trace. Be certain to place the patterns at the same location on both sconces. You might want to measure and mark prior to tracing the pattern. Drill a ¼-inch-diameter hole inside the traced mirror area on both sconces. This hole is for insertion of the saber-saw blade to begin the cutting function. Carefully saw along the

Fig. 3-69. Dimensions for Sconces.

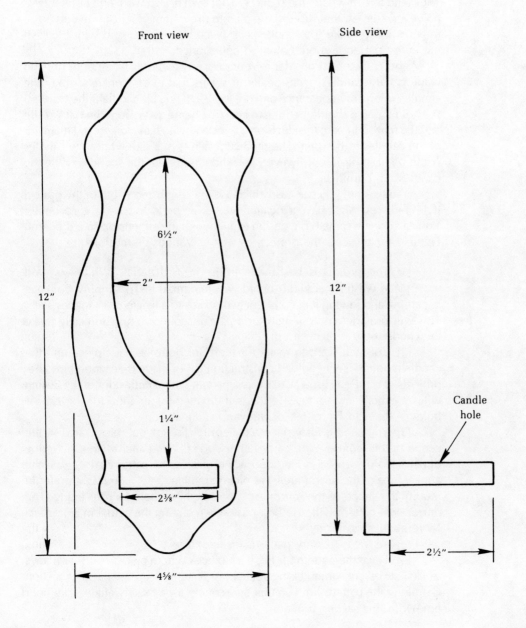

Front view

Side view

6½"

2"

12"

1¼"

2⅜"

4⅝"

12"

Candle hole

2½"

pattern line, especially at the curved ends of the area. Take your time with this procedure so that you have neat edges that will surround the mirror glass. The mirror tends to reflectively expose shoddy sawing. Remember that abrasive paper can remove many minor errors in sawing.

[6] Pattern the two candle holders on scrap material and saw. You want the grain to run lengthwise, front to back edge, on the holders. This makes the holders stronger, but also enhances their appearance.

[7] Drill one hole near the center front edge of each candle-holder piece. As a rule, I drill candle-holder holes using a $^{13}/_{16}$-inch forstner wood bit. This diameter will accept the base of most candles. I have discovered over the years that there is little uniformity in the sizes of candle bases. The average candle base, even though tapered, often ranges in diameter from $^3/_4$ to 1 inch. You might want to use a $^3/_4$-inch-diameter bit and then, if necessary, trim the candle base to fit.

Measure and mark for the holes near the front edge of the holders. Drill the holes to a depth of at least $^5/_8$ inch. Be careful not to drill through the holders.

[8] Rout all edges, including the mirror area on the front surface, using a round-over bit and table-mounted router. Also rout the back edges of the sconces. Rout the candle holders, but do not rout their back edges. You want these sharp edges where they will attach to the back piece.

[9] The mirror glass needs to be recessed in both sconces. To make the recessed area, rout the back edge of the mirror areas using a rabbeting bit. The recess needs to be only deep enough to accommodate standard-thickness mirror glass. Refer to Project 7 for a discussion of routing the recessed area to accommodate mirror glass.

[10] Using a range of abrasive grits, sand all surfaces and edges to finishing readiness. Drill $^1/_4$-inch-diameter hanging holes in the back of both sconces near the top and centered on both sconces. The holes should angle slightly upward so that they will drop over the head of a finishing nail for hanging. Be careful not to drill through the sconce. Take your time when doing this kind of drilling procedure.

[11] Secure the candle holders to the back piece using wood glue and small finishing nails. I generally place the holders at least 1¼ inches below the bottom edge of the mirror area. This placement aligns the holder with the curved extensions on the sides of the back piece. Be certain you measure and mark the location of the holders prior to securing them.

Spread glue on the back edge of the holder and press against the surface of the back piece. Be certain to place it in the premarked location. Allow the glue to dry for a while so that the assembly can be turned over for nailing. The drying glue should keep the holder in place while you drive in the nails. Place the front edge of the holder on a hard surface for the nailing function. Use two nails to secure the holder. If you use only one nail, the glue bond could break under use and the holder would twist. Remove any glue that is forced onto the surface during the assembling process.

[12] The mirror area pattern can be of use in cutting the mirror glass for the sconces. Measure the width of the routed recess in the back piece. With the pattern lying on the mirror glass, place marks around it that reflect the width of the recess. You will need to use a ruler for this procedure. Then cut the mirror glass on the inside edge of these marks. This should result in a mirror that fits exactly into the recess. Refer to Project 7 for a discussion on cutting mirror glass.

Do not glue the mirror into the recess until the sconce is finished with whatever products you plan to use. Cut a piece of construction paper to shape and glue it over the entire back surface as a final procedure.

PROJECT 27: CANDLE HOLDERS

This project is for hanging candle holders that employ commercial candle cups (Fig. 3-70). If desired, you also can use brass rings that fit into the top edge of the candle cups. They give the holders a very professional appearance. The nature of this design and the cups make these holders usable for burning candles. The design is very simple and consistent with an Early American or Country theme.

The project is an ideal one for tole painting. While my own preference is to allow the wood to present itself, the holders do have sufficient surface for a range of tole designs. There is no reason the holders could not be embellished using carving tools or a woodburning unit. You might want to think about various ways that you could enhance the overall appearance of the holders.

The candle holders also lend themselves to a variety of finishes. Rather than staining or using a clear lacquer finish, you might want to paint them to blend in with a room's decor. Pine or country projects do not need to be stained to be attractive. As you will discover in Chapter 4, there are a range of products and methods you can use to enhance your projects.

As with Project 26, you might want to increase the length and width of the holders. Many people seem to enjoy very large candle holders. The sizes suggested in Fig. 3-71 reflect my tastes. You might prefer to significantly alter the overall dimensions to meet a particular need in your household. This opportunity to change designs and dimensions is what makes crafting small projects from pine so much fun. You can, with ease, modify any design to meet specific needs. You can make the projects to accommodate your individual tastes or preferences. As always, do some planning prior to beginning the project. You should also obtain some commercial candle cups and brass rings from one of the mail-order suppliers listed in the Appendix.

[1] In order to make both candle holders, you will need at least 26 inches of 1-×-4 stock for the back pieces and at least 7 inches for the

supports. These lengths allow for some extra wood to make patterning and cutting somewhat easier. You might want to allow a bit more length. As suggested earlier, if you prefer to make the holders longer, simply obtain more 1-×-4 material.

Cut two back pieces to a length of 13 inches and also two support pieces to a length of 3½ inches.

[2] In order for the scroll ends to be neat and balanced in appearance, you would be wise to make patterns. Note in Figs. 3-70 and 3-71 how the ends of the back piece are different on each end. You might prefer to duplicate these shapes rather than designing different ones. The end cuts are somewhat plain, but they maintain the overall simplicity of the holder design.

You can make a pattern of the entire back piece or, if preferred, make two small ones for the ends. Use Fig. 3-71 and the dimensions presented when making a pattern. Use the folded-paper method discussed in earlier projects.

The pattern that is made for the top of the back piece can also be used for the candle support piece. More about this shortly.

[3] Trace the pattern on the two 13-inch pieces and cut. A scroll or saber saw is an effective tool for making the cuts required.

Before tracing the top portion of the pattern onto the support pieces, cut them to a width of 3 inches. Measure and mark a line on the two 3½-inch support pieces and rip them to the required width.

Trace the top back piece design on one end of each support piece. Using a saber saw, cut along the pattern lines on both pieces.

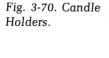

Fig. 3-70. Candle Holders.

[4] Because the candle holders are hung on nails, you will need to drill a ¼-inch-hole in the top center of both back pieces. Measure and mark the center of the pieces before drilling the holes. Refer to Fig. 3-71 for the placement of the hanging holes. A counterbore bit will flair the edges of the drilled holes and give them a more finished appearance. You can also use

Fig. 3-71. Dimensions for Candle Holders.

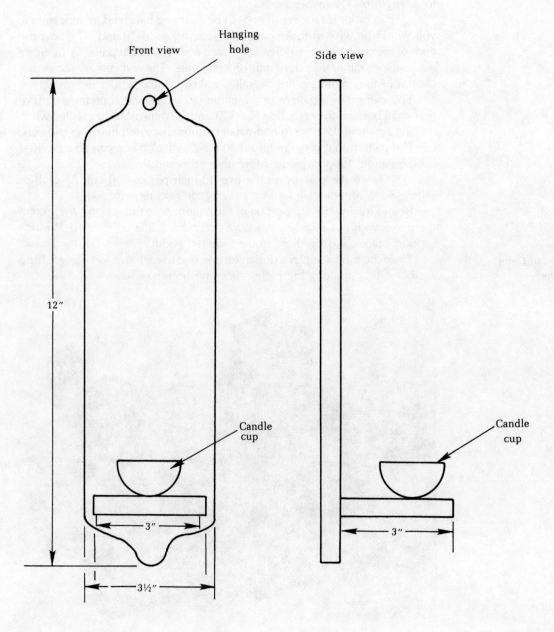

a standard ¼-inch-diameter high-speed bit. Drill the two holes in the same location on both back pieces.

[5] Rout all edges on the back piece using a round-over bit and a table-mounted router. Don't overrout these edges. Rout the candle support pieces on the top, bottom, and front edges. Do not rout the back edges of the support. These edges need to be sharp for attachment to the surface of the back piece.

[6] Using a range of abrasive grits, sand all surfaces and edges to a finishing readiness. Be certain to sand with the grain of the wood. Spend some extra time sanding the front edges of the candle support pieces. They are highly visible when the holders are hung and they should be relatively smooth.

[7] The candle support pieces should be glued and nailed to the back pieces before the candle cups are secured. This procedure makes the attachment of these pieces much easier.

Measure and mark the exact location of the support pieces on the front surface of the back piece. Spread wood glue on the surface of the back edge of both supports and place them on the back pieces. Allow the glue to begin to dry before you begin nailing. Once the glue is dry enough to hold the supports in place, turn the assembly over and nail the support pieces in place. Use two finishing nails to secure each support piece. You can drive the nails in while the front edge of the candle support piece is resting against a hard surface. Wipe away any excess glue. Refer to Fig. 3-71 to note the correct placement of the support pieces on the back pieces.

[8] Secure the candle cups near the front edge of the support pieces using both wood glue and small finishing nails. Spread a dab of wood glue on the bottom area of the candle cups and place them on the support pieces. Be certain they are both centered and in approximately the same location on the support pieces. The entire holder should be standing upright during this procedure so that the cups do not slide on the glue. Allow the glue to partially dry.

When the glue is sufficiently dry to hold the candle cups in place, turn the assembly over and place the top edge of the cup on a hard surface. Drive a small finishing nail from the bottom surface of the support piece into the candle cup. Place the nail so that it will penetrate the center of the bottom surface of the candle cup.

PROJECT 28: GOOSE CANDLE HOLDER

The Goose Candle Holder (Fig. 3-72) is representative of a range of designs that can be made to hold small candles. To give these projects more stability, a small base is added to them. Whenever projects are to employ candles, it is critical that they be designed and made in a way that they will not easily tip over. The candles that are used in this type of project are those generally used for angel chimes. Their base diameter is approximately ⁷⁄₁₆ inch.

You will find that Project 30 presents a variety of ornament designs that can be easily enlarged to be small candle holders. In addition to these designs, there is no end of possibilities for use in making small candle holders. To enhance the project further, these small holders present sufficient surface for tole painting. They can also be painted in a variety of colors. As you plan the project, consider some of the many options that are available for enhancing the holder.

Figure 3-73 presents the outline of the Goose Candle Holder, as well as its dimensions. You might want to vary either the shape or the dimensions of the project. Do some design work prior to beginning work on the project. You will want to make a pattern for the project so integrate your own ideas into the design.

[1] You will need at least 6 inches of standard 1-×-6 stock for the goose. The base can be made from a piece of scrap 1-inch stock. It is 3 inches long and 2 inches wide. If you place your goose pattern properly on the 6-inch-wide stock, you can make two holders from the same board.

[2] Make a goose pattern using construction paper. Refer to Fig. 3-73 for the approximate dimensions of the project. Trace the pattern on the stock and cut using a saber saw. Cut the base piece from a piece of scrap.

[3] Sand all surfaces and edges using various abrasive grits. You want the project to be ready for finishing.

[4] Use wood glue to secure the goose to the base. Drive a finishing nail up through the bottom surface of the base into the foot section of the

Fig. 3-72. Goose
Candle Holder.

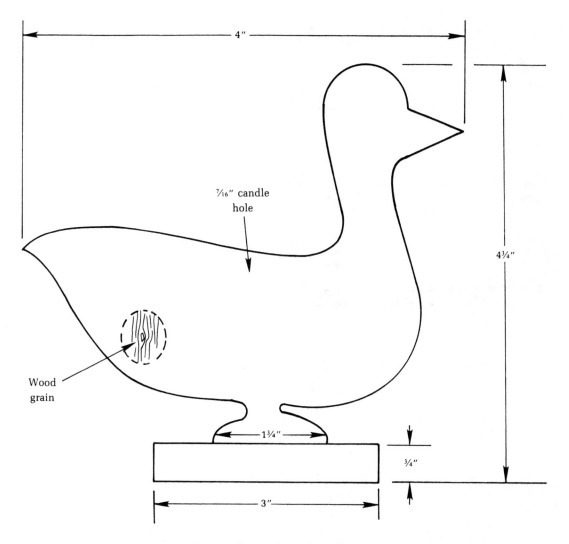

4"

⁷⁄₁₆" candle
hole

4¾"

Wood
grain

1¾"

¾"

3"

Fig. 3-73. Dimensions
for Goose Candle
Holder.

goose. Use a nail punch to drive the nail's head below the surface.

[5] Drill the candle hole into the center back of the goose. I use a ⁷⁄₁₆-inch-diameter high-speed steel bit, but you might want to use something a bit larger or smaller. Depending upon the manufacturer, there is some difference in the base diameter of the small angel chime candles. Drill the hole to a depth of at least ⅜ inch.

PROJECT 29: ANGEL CANDLE HOLDER

The project (Fig. 3-74) is an example of a small candle holder for the Christmas season. It represents how almost any design can be made to function as a

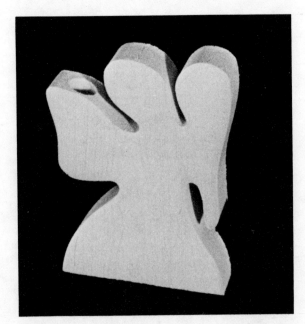

Fig. 3-74. Angel Candle Holder.

Hole for candle

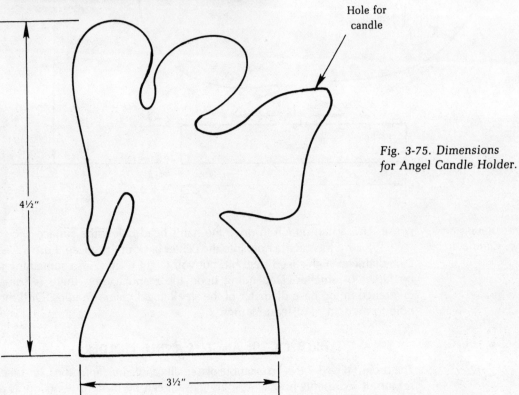

Fig. 3-75. Dimensions for Angel Candle Holder.

4½"

3½"

small decorative holder. For example, a similar holder could be made using a teddy bear, rabbit, cat, or any other animal or object. This design presents ample surface for a variety of tole-painted or other designs.

As with Project 28, this design requires a small, angel chime-type candle. A 7/16-inch-diameter hole is drilled in the top edge of the hand area to hold the candle. The candle holder can easily be made from 5-inch-long scraps of 1-×-4 material.

Figure 3-75 presents an outline of the project, along with suggested dimensions. Refer to Project 28 for specific tasks for making the holder.

PROJECT 30: CHRISTMAS TREE ORNAMENTS

One of my favorite small pine projects is the designing and making of small wooden Christmas tree ornaments (Fig. 3-76). Over the years, I've developed about 50 different ornament designs. A few of these designs are presented in Fig. 3-77 to give you some ideas on the range of ornaments that can be designed and cut. The possible designs for ornaments are endless.

In addition to having a good time designing and cutting the ornaments, they are great fun to paint or burn. Pine lends itself to almost any kind of paint. The ornaments can also be decorated with children's felt-tipped pens, color crayons, water colors and, obviously, paints used by the tole painter. The ornaments make for great family or school projects.

You can make the ornaments from 1-inch-thick scrap material that is salvaged from other projects. Most of the designs are no more than 3 inches long and 2½ inches wide. These dimensions can obviously be varied to suit

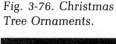
Fig. 3-76. Christmas Tree Ornaments.

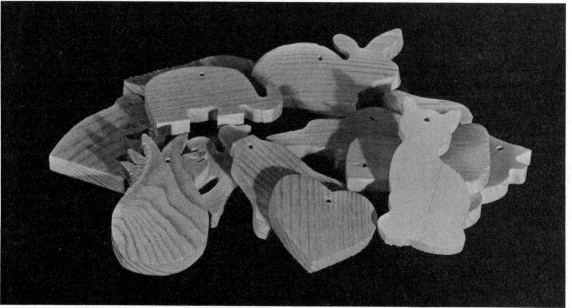

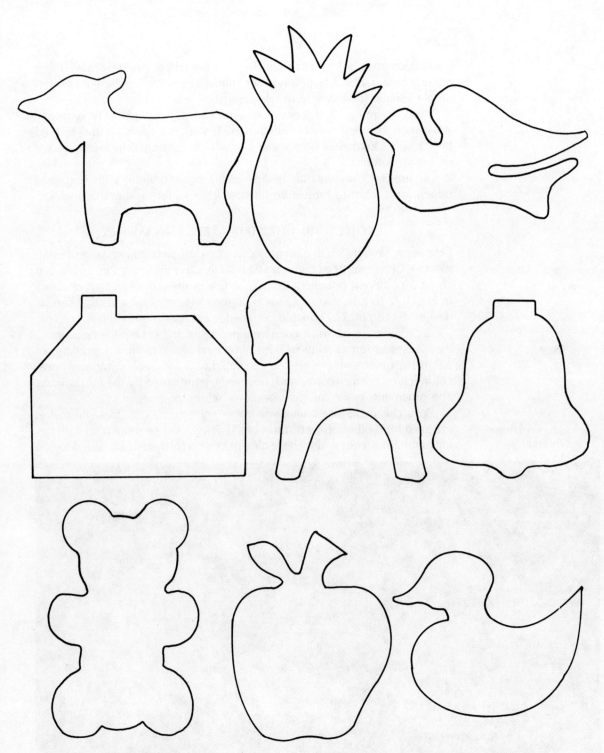

Fig. 3-77. Ornament patterns.

a particular design or project need. I have developed the habit of saving almost every usable scrap that results from other projects. Those pieces that can't be used for wood ornaments are excellent for the fireplace or wood-burning stove.

You will definitely want to make patterns for each ornament design. While you can make the initial patterns from construction paper, you can use the actual ornaments for subsequent patterning needs. The process of developing a design and making a pattern can be a very challenging experience. Although the design might look like a given object to you, others might quickly disagree. It can be difficult to develop a pattern that actually resembles something.

Although the ornaments are initially patterned and cut from standard 1-inch-thick stock, I rip the finished ornament into two pieces. This resawing procedure results in two exact ornaments that are approximately ⅜ inch thick each. The ornaments are also considerably lighter in weight, when cut, for hanging on a tree. These thinner designs can also be used for key rings, curtain pulls, wreath decorations, name tags, gift tags, kitchen magnets, and any number of other functional and decorative purposes. In order for the ornaments to have a smooth finished surface on both sides, sand the surface that has been resawed. A belt sander is the ideal tool for sanding the ornaments.

You can cut the various ornament designs from the patterns using a saber saw or a floor-model scroll saw. One of the many new floor-model scroll saws is the ideal tool for cutting small ornaments. In my shop, I use a 24-inch Delta scroll saw. Sawing a single ornament into two ornaments is best done using a band saw with a ½-inch-wide blade.

Unless the ornaments are to be used for kitchen magnets, drill holes through them for hanging. The holes need to be drilled near the top center edge of the ornament. Centering the hole properly is critical. The ornaments will not hang straight if the holes are not properly centered. You might need to experiment to find the exact point for drilling the hanging holes. The holes only need to be large enough to accommodate a small piece of string. If you are using key chains, drill the hole diameter to a size that will accommodate the chain.

PROJECT 31: HANGING CANDLE SHELF

This project is a small shelf that can be used to display a candle and its holder or a collectible (Fig. 3-78). Its decorative scrollwork makes it an attractive piece for hanging in any room. If you prefer, you can make the shelf into a candle holder. You can secure a commercial candle cup to the front center surface of the shelf piece. If the hanging shelf is used for candles, exercise caution to place the candle away from the sides and back piece. There must be sufficient distance between the flame and any wood surface.

Although the project can be made from standard ¾-inch-thick stock, it is best crafted from ½-inch-thick material. The size of the design lends itself to using thinner stock. If you prefer using thicker stock, you might want to increase the overall dimensions of the project. Add at least 1 inch to all project dimensions. Figure 3-79 presents the design and approximate dimensions for making the project from ½-inch-thick stock. To assist you in your design and planning, Fig. 3-80 presents a side view and dimensions of the project.

[1] The project requires at least 3 feet of 1-×-6 material that is sawed or planed to a ½-inch thickness. If you have a band saw, you can use a ½-inch-wide blade for resawing stock to the desired thickness. You will want to sand the sawed surface to remove the saw marks left by the blade. As indicated, if you do not have access to ½-inch-thick stock, you can craft the project from standard ¾-inch-thick material. Simply add at least 1 inch to all the suggested dimensions.

[2] For the back piece, cut a piece of material that is at least 10 inches long. In order for the top scrollwork to be balanced, it is best to make a pattern. Using a piece of construction paper that is exactly 5½ inches wide (the width of a 1-×-6 board), fold the paper in half. While referring to the various illustrations, draw half of the scroll design on the upper portion of the folded construction paper. Using a scissors, cut out the traced area. This will give you, when opened, a pattern that has the exact scroll design on both sides of the folded paper. You might prefer an alternative design. Try your hand at designing a scroll more to your own liking. Much of the fun in making pine projects is to use your own design ideas.

Trace the pattern on the surface of the back piece. Be certain that the pattern is placed so that the length of the back piece will be 9 inches. Then

Fig. 3-78. Hanging Candle Shelf.

144

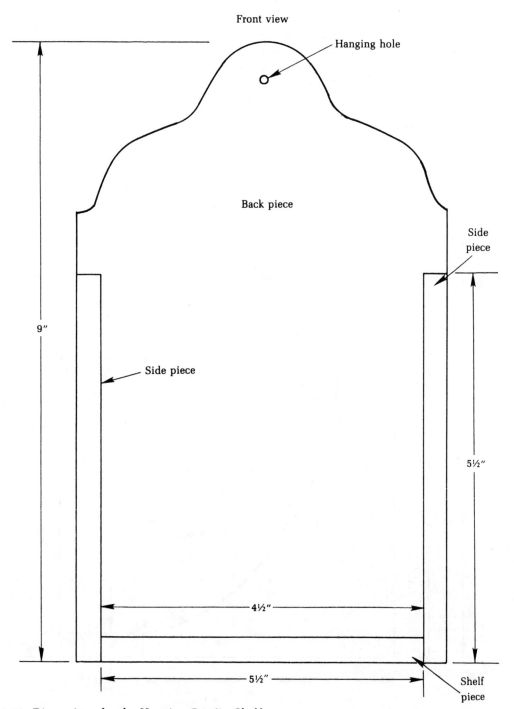

Front view

Hanging hole

Back piece

Side piece

Side piece

Shelf piece

9"

5½"

4½"

5½"

Fig. 3-79. Dimensions for the Hanging Candle Shelf.

cut out the scroll pattern using a scroll saw and a finishing blade. Take your time with the sawing and carefully follow the traced line.

[3] Mark the center of the back piece near the top of the scroll and drill a ¼-inch-diameter hanging hole. The drilled hole should be large enough to accommodate the head of a finishing nail that would be used for hanging.

Fig. 3-80. Side view of the Hanging Candle Shelf.

Side view

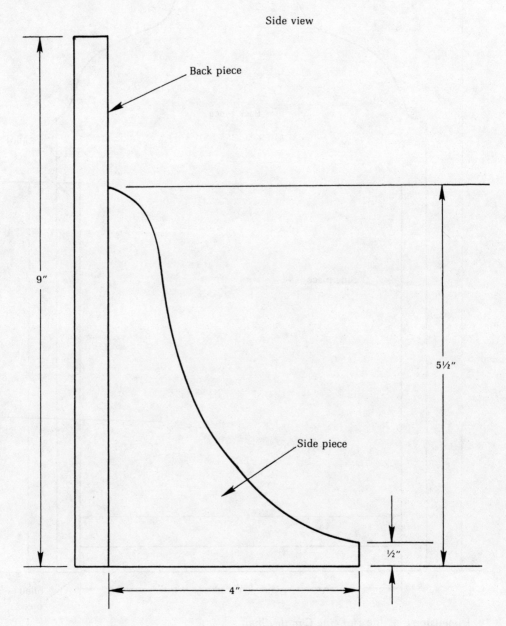

[4] Next, prepare the two side pieces. Cut two pieces of stock that are approximately 6 inches long and exactly 4 inches wide. Refer to Fig. 3-80 to note the design and dimensions of the side pieces.

Rather than making a pattern from paper, it is best to design and cut one side piece, then use it as a pattern for making the second side piece. You can easily draw the curved front edge of the side piece onto the surface freehand. Note that the front bottom edge of the side piece is ½ inch wide. This width allows the ends of the side pieces to be flush with the shelf piece. If you are using thicker stock, this area would be ¾ inch wide. It must match the thickness of the shelf piece.

Pattern and cut the two side pieces using a scroll saw and a finishing blade. Take your time with the cutting process so that you have smooth, even front edges on the two pieces.

[5] The final component that needs to be prepared is the actual shelf piece. This piece needs to be 4 inches long and 4½ inches wide. Cut and measure the piece carefully as you will want a good fit.

[6] Using a range of abrasive grits, sand all surfaces of the various parts to a finishing readiness. If desired, you can lightly roll all exposed edges using a table-mounted router and a round-over bit. If you decide to rout the edges, be certain that the depth of cut of the bit is not set too deeply. Test the cut with some scrap material before you rout the actual shelf components.

Frequently when using ½-inch-thick stock, I simply round the exposed edges using abrasive paper. You need only sand the sharpness from the edges. This is an effective alternative to routing the edges.

[7] Assemble the project using small finishing nails and wood glue. First, assemble the two side pieces to the shelf piece. Be certain that the nails are centered so that they don't split out portions of the shelf piece. Also, wipe away any glue that squeezes from the joints.

Secure the side pieces and shelf piece to the back piece. Drive finishing nails from the back surface of the shelf piece into the back edges of the side pieces. Remove any excess glue from the various surfaces.

[8] If you prefer making the project into a self-contained candle holder, attach a commercial candle cup to the front center surface of the shelf piece. Secure the candle cup to the surface using glue and a small finishing nail driven from the bottom surface of the shelf piece into the cup.

PROJECT 32: LETTER HOLDER

A very functional project and one that brings order to an otherwise disorderly process is the Letter Holder (Fig. 3-81). This project is well suited for those households where letters and other important documents tend to be misplaced. It can be easily hung on the end of a cabinet, on a wall, near the telephone, or in some other conspicuous location where it is easily accessible. If you do not wish to be reminded of correspondence or accumulating bills, the holder can be secured in a less conspicuous location. Regardless of where it is hung, the letter holder will provide a mechanism for holding important materials.

This project presents considerable surface for tole painting or some other type of decorative enhancement. In addition to three panel surfaces, the sides of the holder present ample area for any desired embellishments. If you are not into tole painting or stenciling, you might want to consider carving or woodburning some kind of design onto the surfaces. My preference is to either stain or finish the project with a clear lacquer finish, omitting any embellishments.

Although the project can be made from standard ¾-inch-thick stock, portions of it are best made using ½-inch-thick material. When standard thickness material is used throughout the project, it tends to become rather heavy and also very bulky looking. The thicker stock also tends to limit the amount of letters and other papers that can be held in the various pockets. As you will discover in the various tasks, if you are unable to purchase ½-inch-thick stock, you can easily resaw it on a band saw.

Figure 3-82 presents a front view of the project, along with some approximate dimensions. This drawing assumes the use of ½-inch-thick material for the side pieces and the panels.

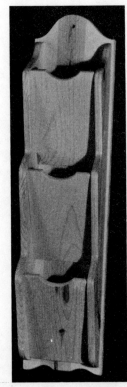

Fig. 3-81. Letter Holder.

[1] The project is best made from 1-×-6 material. For the back piece of the holder, you will need approximately 2½ feet of stock. The actual length of the back piece is only 23½ inches, but the extra material makes both patterning and cutting a bit easier. You can also make the two side pieces and three panels from 1-×-6 stock. As indicated, you will need to resaw the standard thickness down to a ½-inch thickness. This procedure can easily be done using a ½-inch-wide band-saw blade. Other alternatives are to purchase ½-inch-thick stock or plane standard ¾-inch-thick material down to the desired thickness. If you plan to saw your own material or plane it down, you will need at least 6 feet of 1-×-6 stock. If you plan to buy stock already planed to ½-inch thickness, you also will need about 6 feet of stock for the sides and panels.

[2] Measure, pattern both ends, and cut the back piece from ¾-inch-thick 1-×-6 material. Refer to Fig. 3-82 to note the scroll designs on the top and bottom of the back piece. While I'm inclined to rather simple designs, you might prefer something a bit more elaborate. If you are unable to draw the two designs freehand onto the wood's surface, you can make patterns for both the top and bottom. Refer to the earlier discussions on pattern-making for the necessary procedures. You can easily cut the patterned scroll area using a saber saw and the appropriate blade. Locate the center of the back piece near the top and drill a ⅛-inch-diameter hole for hanging the unit.

[3] Patterning and cutting the two side pieces are probably the most difficult tasks in the project. You will need ½-inch-thick stock of ample length

Front view

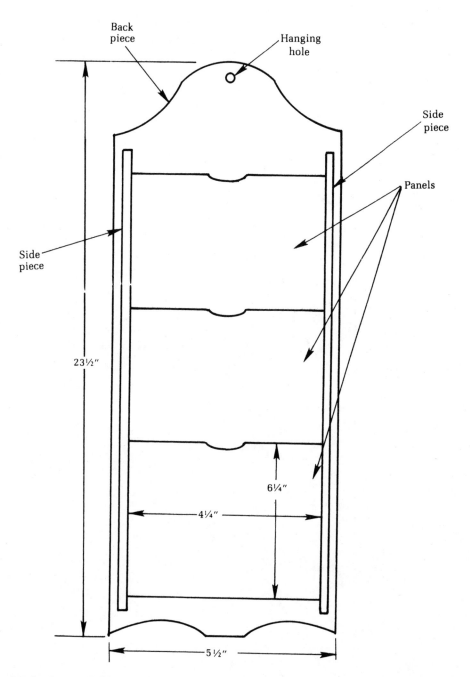

Fig. 3-82. Dimensions for the Letter Holder.

for the two side pieces (Fig. 3-83) presents both a design and approximate dimensions.

Rather than make a separate pattern, an effective procedure is to draw the design directly onto one of the side pieces. Cut a piece of ½-inch stock to a length of at least 24 inches. While this length will result in some waste, it makes both patterning and cutting a bit easier. Using Fig. 3-83 as your design and dimensional guide, draw the exact outline of the side panel onto the surface of the piece. The three dimensions that need to be constant are

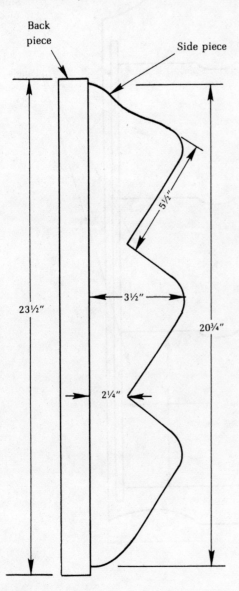

Fig. 3-83. Side view of the Letter Holder.

indicated in Fig. 3-83. As you will note, the top and bottom ends of the piece are somewhat different. Pattern them accordingly onto the board's surface.

When the patterning process is complete, use a scroll saw to cut out the patterned piece along the penciled lines. Take your time cutting so that the curves are the same and the straight edges are straight. The side pieces are very visible when the holder is hung, so you want them to be as neat as possible.

Using the one cut side piece as a pattern, trace it onto another piece cut to length. Be certain to align the back edges of both pieces before tracing. After carefully tracing the pattern, cut out the second side piece. Be certain to cut on the traced line.

If you sawed the side-piece material on the band saw, you might have two rather rough surfaces. Depending upon the type of blade used, you might want to sand the surfaces smooth. Be careful not to remove too much wood, especially near the edges. You will want to use an electric finishing sander or a large floor-model sander for this procedure.

[4] You need to prepare three panels from ½-inch-thick stock. Figure 3-84 presents both the design and dimensions of the panels. When cutting the panels, be certain the wood grain runs up and down on all three. You might want to pattern and saw the cutout area on one panel and then trace it onto the other two panels. This procedure will ensure that the three panel cutouts are exactly the same.

If the panels have one rough surface from being sawed on the band saw, sanding is not necessary. Simply place the rough surface to the inside when the panels are assembled. The rough surfaces will never be seen.

[5] Using a round-over bit and a table-mounted router, round-over all exposed edges slightly. Do not rout the bottom edges of the side pieces, nor the sides of the panels. Remember, those edges that will be joined to another surface should not be routed.

When routing stock that is only ½ inch thick, you must use extra care in setting the depth of cut of the router bit. The cut cannot be too deep or it will cut through the thinner stock. Make a few practice routes with scrap material before you do the final routing on the side pieces and the panels.

[6] Using a range of abrasive grits, bring all exposed surfaces to finishing readiness. You should also lightly sand the various routed edges. In general, prepare all the surfaces and edges for the finishing process. By way of information, I frequently stain the various pieces before assembling them. This makes the staining process much easier. If you plan to stain your project, you might want to consider doing it prior to assembly.

[7] To assemble the holder, the side pieces and the three panels are first assembled as a unit. The assembled unit is then attached to the back piece. You will want to use wood glue and finishing nails for the assembling tasks. Figure 3-85 indicates how the panels are placed on the side surface of a side piece.

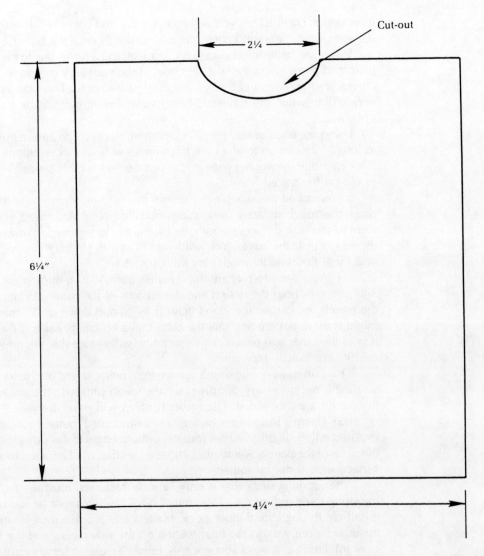

Cut-out

2¼

6¼"

4¼"

Secure the panels to one side piece at a time. Generally I secure the top panel first. Spread glue on the side edge of the panel and place it on the inside surface of the side piece. The inside bottom edge of the panel should be flush with the bottom edge of the side piece. Align the top corner of the panel so that it is near the extended curve in the top piece. This is an eyeball procedure. After the panel has been properly placed, turn the assembly over so that you can nail through the side piece and into the edge of the panel. Check the alignment of the panel before you drive the nails. Also, be certain that the nails will penetrate the middle of the panel edge. While this is an awkward procedure, it can be done. Repeat the process with the other two panels.

Fig. 3-84. Front view of a panel for the Letter Holder.

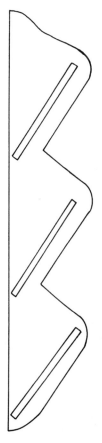

Fig. 3-85. *Side view of a panel for the Letter Holder.*

After the three panels have been secured to one side piece, spread glue on the other three panel edges. You might want to align and nail the panels with both side pieces placed on their back edges to ensure that the side pieces are aligned with one another. This is important when you attach the back piece to the assembled section. After the panels have been nailed to both side pieces, use a nail punch to drive the nail heads slightly under the wood's surface.

[8] Spread wood glue on the bottom edges of the two side pieces and place the assembled section onto the front surface of the back piece. Place the assembled section carefully, being certain that it is dimensionally balanced on all four sides of the back piece. You want it reasonably centered on the back piece.

When the assembled section is in place, turn the entire assembly over and place it face down on a hard surface. Be careful that the assembled section does not slide on the surface of the back piece during this procedure. Using finishing nails, secure the back piece to the assembled section. Place the nails so that they will penetrate into the middle of the bottom edge of the side piece. You don't want the nails splitting out the sides of the side pieces. Place a nail about every 3 inches on both sides along the length of the side pieces. This, along with the glue, will assure you of a solid assembly. Wipe off any excess glue that squeezes out during the assembly process.

PROJECT 33: LARGE OPEN CABINET

For those who need a large, functional display cabinet, the Open Cabinet (Fig. 3-86) is an ideal project. Its size makes it usable for displaying collectibles and other items that you might want to showcase. The project design utilizes dimensions that allow for a range of sizes in items to be placed on the shelves. While the suggested project dimensions will accommodate a range of collectibles in different sizes, you might want to alter the dimensions to meet specific needs.

In addition to designing the cabinet to hold particular types of items, you can modify the dimensions to place the cabinet in a specific place. After you have determined the wall location where you want the cabinet hung, do some measuring to assist you in making the cabinet. While specific dimensions are provided for the project, you might want it larger or slightly smaller to meet your needs. You might prefer to double the length of the cabinet in order to display a collection of items together. As suggested earlier, you also might want to vary the number and space between the shelves in order to accommodate particular items.

To assist you in your planning activities, Fig. 3-87 presents the large open cabinet project, along with appropriate dimensions.

[1] The Large Open Cabinet is made from 1-×-6 stock. The top and bottom pieces along with the two side pieces are made from 1-×-6 stock of standard thickness. If you have a band saw, you can rip the shelves from standard stock to a thickness of ⅜ to ½ inch. A band saw will also be helpful in ripping the back boards of the cabinet to a thickness of ¼ inch. If you do not have a band saw, you can use one of various alternatives to make the shelves and the back boards. They will be discussed shortly.

To make the cabinet frame and shelves, you will need a minimum of 10 feet of standard 1-×-6 stock. This does not include any material for the back boards, but does allow for some waste. It also assumes that you will be using only two shelves in your design. If your planned design calls for more shelves or a larger overall cabinet frame, increase the amount of 1-×-6 material accordingly.

Using Fig. 3-87 and its dimensions as a guide, measure and cut the various

Fig. 3-86. Large Open Cabinet.

pieces required for the project. First cut all pieces to length. To give the overall project a more attractive appearance, the side pieces are narrower than the top and bottom pieces. Also, the shelves are narrower than the side pieces. If all of the pieces were cut and assembled in the same width, the cabinet would look very boxlike and rather unattractive. Staggering the width of the various pieces greatly enhances the overall appearance of the cabinet.

Figure 3-88 presents the various widths of the cabinet pieces. Use these dimensions as your guide when ripping the various pieces. If a band saw is not available for ripping the various pieces to their proper width, you can use a scroll saw.

[2] If you have a band saw, rip the two shelf pieces to a thickness of ⅜ to ½ inch. Overall appearance tends to be enhanced if the shelf pieces are cut to one of these thicknesses; however, if a band saw is not available, the shelves can be used with their standard ¾-inch thickness. You might prefer the appearance and the stability of the thicker shelves.

[3] Rout selected edges on all the cabinet pieces using a round-over bit and a table-mounted router. Do not rout the back edges of the shelves. Also, do not round-over the back inside edges of the top and bottom pieces and the two side pieces. These four edges require grooves to be routed in

Fig. 3-87. Dimensions of the Large Open Cabinet.

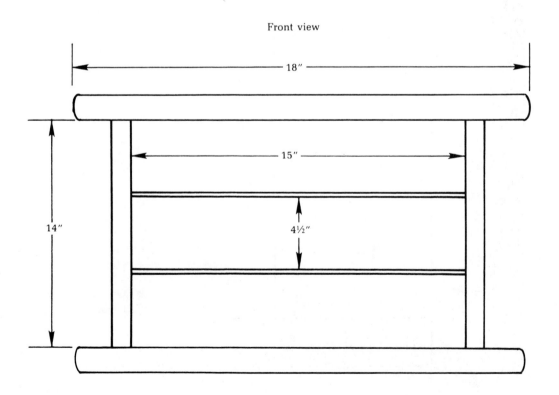

Front view

18″

15″

14″

4½″

155

them with a rabbeting bit. It is these routed grooves that hold the back boards in place and allow the entire back surface of the cabinet to be flush. More about this shortly.

Using a round-over router bit, rout the two front edges of the shelves. Rout the front edges and one back edge on both side pieces. On the top and bottom piece, rout the two front edges, the end edges, and one edge on the

Fig. 3-88. Side view of the Large Open Cabinet.

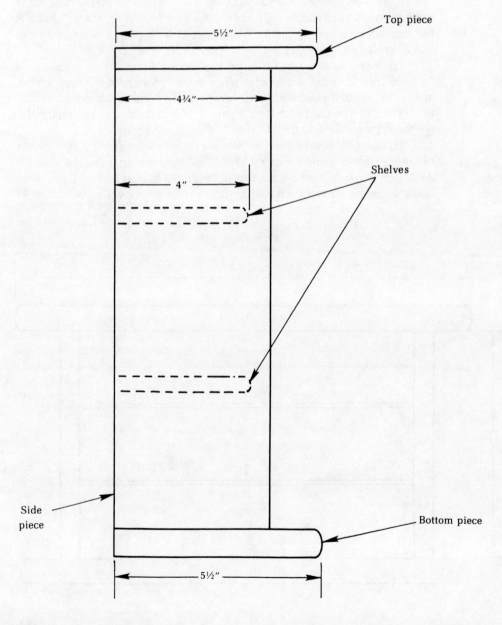

back of each piece. You shouldn't rout edges that will be joined to another surface. Thus, you should not round the end edges of the two side pieces of the cabinet.

[4] Using a rabbeting bit in a table-mounted router, rout a groove in the back edges of the two side pieces and the top and bottom piece. Make the groove on those edges that were not rounded-over in the earlier procedure. Remember, it is in these grooves that the back pieces of the cabinet will eventually be secured. Determine the depth of the grooves by the thickness of the back pieces or the plywood that you are using. While ¼-inch-thick strips or plywood make for a strong cabinet, a thickness of ⅛ inch is acceptable.

Rout the various grooves in relation to the planned thickness of the back board. Do not attempt to rout too deeply at a single pass with a rabbeting bit. Make shallow cuts and a number of passes. A rabbeting bit can be rather dangerous if you attempt to make the cut too deep in a single pass.

Figure 3-89 indicates where the rabbeted grooves are on the assembled cabinet frame. Note that the grooves are rabbeted the entire length of the two side pieces, but not on the top and bottom pieces.

[5] Using a range of abrasive papers, sand all the edges and surfaces to a finishing readiness. As with any project that will be assembled, it is much easier to do the sanding work before assembly. Do a thorough job, especially on the surfaces of all pieces.

[6] The side pieces and the top and bottom pieces must be assembled first. You will want to use both wood glue and some appropriate size finishing nails. You would be well advised to use the floor or a large surface for assembling the cabinet. It is somewhat easier to assemble the parts if they are placed on their back edges.

In order to ensure that the side pieces are assembled so that they will accommodate the shelves, use a shelf piece as a guide. You want the shelves to fit snugly between the two side pieces. Place the shelf pieces, unsecured, near the ends of the side pieces as the top and bottom pieces are being secured to them. The procedure is somewhat awkward, but well worth the effort. If you will reflect briefly on the procedure, you will see the necessity for it.

Spread wood glue on the ends of the side pieces, place a shelf between them, and set the top piece in place. Be certain the rabbeted grooves on all pieces are placed to the inside back. As suggested, you want to do this assembly procedure with the various pieces placed on their back edges on the floor or a large, flat surface. You also want the top piece to extend an equal distance from the outer surfaces of the side pieces. The overlap of the top piece should be the same distance on both sides.

While abutting the side pieces to the bottom surface of the top piece with a shelf in place, drive finishing nails through the top piece and into the side pieces. Be certain that the side pieces are snug against the ends of the shelf guide before you drive in the nails. You want the shelves to fit snugly between the side pieces.

Reverse the process and secure the bottom piece to the other ends of the side pieces. Again, use a shelf as a guide. Be certain that the overlap on the bottom piece is the same as on the top piece. To note how the overlap appears on the finished cabinet, refer to Fig. 3-87.

It is important to remember that the back edges of the side pieces and the top and bottom pieces are all flush. This is assured if you assemble the unit while it is lying on its back. Take your time with these procedures. Think through each step before driving in any nails. Remember to have the routed grooves on the back inside edges of all the pieces. These grooves will hold the back pieces, so it is critical that you place them correctly. Wipe off any excess glue that is forced onto the surfaces.

[7] Using a nail punch, drive the heads of the finishing nails slightly

Fig. 3-89. Back view of the Large Open Cabinet.

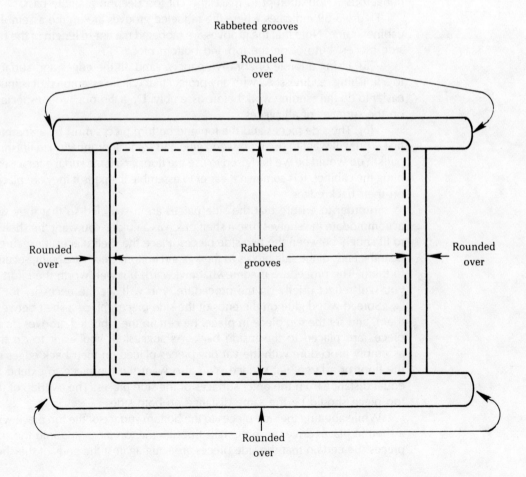

Rabbeted grooves

Rounded over

Rounded over

Rabbeted grooves

Rounded over

Rounded over

Rounded over

under the surfaces of the top and bottom pieces.

[8] To simplify securing the shelves inside the cabinet frame, cut two pieces of scrap material to a length of about 4¼ inches. Place these two pieces, with the cabinet standing upright, against the inside surfaces of the side pieces (Fig. 3-90). Then place the shelf on top of the two pieces for nailing in place. The length of the two scrap pieces will determine the space between the shelves. You might want to vary the space between the shelves by simply using scrap pieces of different lengths.

[9] If the shelf piece fits snugly between the side pieces, with the scrap pieces in place, turn the assembly onto its side. The back edge of the shelf should be flush with the inside edge of the routed grooves to permit the back boards to fit tightly against the back edges of the shelves.

While the assembly is on its side and the shelf is resting on the scrap pieces, drive two finishing nails through the side piece and into the end of the shelf. Be certain to place the nails properly so that they will enter the center portion of the shelf end. Repeat the procedure on the other side of the assembly. For securing the second shelf, repeat the procedures.

Fig. 3-90. Front view of the Large Open Cabinet.

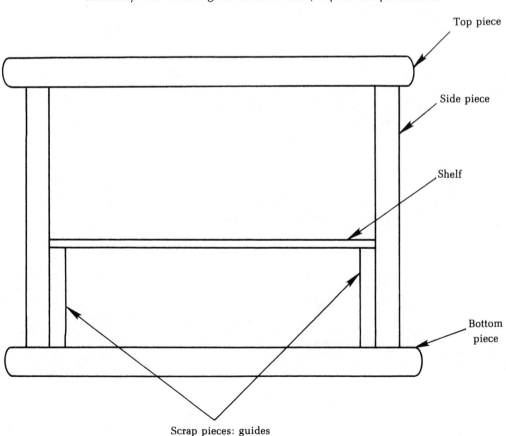

Top piece

Side piece

Shelf

Bottom piece

Scrap pieces: guides

I seldom use wood glue on the ends of the shelves. The nails are usually adequate to hold the shelves in place. When glue is spread on the ends of the shelves, it tends to smear all over the inside surfaces of the side pieces when they are put in place. If you prefer using glue in addition to the nails, be certain you remove any glue that gets smeared around on these inside surfaces.

[10] After the shelves are in place, prepare the back pieces that fit inside the routed grooves. You might prefer to use plywood. As indicated, if you have a band saw, it is relatively easy to cut strips of wood to an appropriate width and thickness for use as back pieces. The strips should be at least 1 inch wide. The width of the strips is determined by the depth of the rabbeted grooves. Usually, you will need to cut one final strip of a different width to complete the backing. The strips should, of course, run up and down on the back surface.

Measure the length of the strips needed from the outer edges of the routed grooves. The actual measured width between the side pieces will determine how many strips you will need. Secure the strips in place using wood glue and small wire brads driven into the routed grooves.

If you use plywood, simply measure the internal dimensions of the back area and cut the plywood accordingly. Remember to measure to the edges of the routed grooves so that the plywood can be properly secured in place. You also can secure the plywood using wood glue and brads. Be certain to have the grain of the plywood running up and down when you place the plywood in the grooves. This is for appearance only.

To simplify the finishing process, do not secure the strips in place until everything has been finished, especially if you plan to stain the cabinet. Staining is much easier if the back strips are not in place.

Chapter 4

Finishing and Hanging Projects

Finishing pine projects and then hanging or placing them in appropriate locations in the house are also part of the woodworking process. Many people, including myself, prefer the actual crafting process. Finishing and hanging the pieces, however, are mandatory tasks and, despite any aversion to these procedures, you must do them.

As you no doubt are aware, the chemical industry has inundated the marketplace with finishing products. Although this variety greatly facilitates the finishing process, it also serves to confuse and often discourage the beginning woodworker. The selection of stains or paints often involves a rather tedious decision-making process. The plethora of oils, lacquers, varnishes, and polyurethanes often serves only to confuse. Although I encourage you to explore this incredible world of chemistry, I also suggest you consider using a few products that I have found helpful. After finishing pine projects for many years, I have identified a number of products and developed a few useful finishing methods.

Much progress also has been made in developing very functional devices to hang projects. Although a finishing nail driven into the wall is still an effective method, there are numerous alternatives to this hanging procedure. I will present a number of useful devices and methods to assist you in hanging the range of pine projects that you have crafted.

The major problem in hanging any piece is deciding on its location. Although the crafting process can be filled with great satisfaction, the hanging process can be fraught with grief. Seldom, if ever, have two individuals agreed on the exact location of any item in a household. Compounding the process are ancillary issues, such as whether the piece is too high or too low, or whether it is straight or crooked. Although I can assist you in learning about the devices and methods for hanging projects, you are on your own in resolving relational problems that develop. My best recommendation is to learn how to hang pieces and then hang them when no one else is around. This approach has worked well in my household.

REASONS FOR FINISHING

There are two basic reasons for putting some type of finish on the projects that you have crafted. First, wood needs to be protected. This protection is especially important for projects that are placed in the bathroom or other areas where they will be exposed to excessive moisture. Although you cannot make wood waterproof with household-type finishes, you can give it sufficient protection to minimize damage.

The protective function of finishing also serves to protect the wood from other products that would stain or mark it. Chemicals in soaps, alcohol, and a variety of other liquids can stain the wood unless there is some type of finish on its surface. Finishes, especially surface-type finishes, also make cleaning or dusting wood pieces considerably easier. One of the disadvantages of oil-type finishes is that, if not applied properly, they tend to collect dust and are difficult to keep clean.

The second reason for finishing wood projects is decorative. Fortunately, most modern finishing products are manufactured to serve both a protective and decorative function. It is the decorative function, however, that confronts the would-be finisher with the most problems. The selection of colors, whether paint or stain, can be most frustrating. Although they often look appropriate on a manufacturer's color chart, their appearance seems to change radically when they are applied to wood.

An effective procedure in selecting colors is to simply purchase the smallest quantity available and test it on a scrap of wood. Although this procedure is usually effective, it often results in a collection of small cans of unwanted stains and paints. When you are doing this type of testing, it is important to remember that pine soaks up both stain and paint very easily. Unlike hardwoods, pine is not always the easiest wood to finish. Its porosity can greatly distort colors, especially with stains.

Tole painters also must decide on finishing products that are compatible with the paints to be used. It is imperative that, if you plan to tole-paint your projects, you check with a tole painter about finishing products. You also might want to review some of the books listed in the Bibliography.

PRELIMINARIES TO FINISHING

Before you apply any finishing products, you must properly prepare the wood's surface. For most pine projects, you must adequately sand the wood and remove all dust. The quality of the final finish is primarily determined by how well the surface has been sanded.

Prior to final sanding of the surfaces, you might want to fill nail holes, cracks, or other areas with a wood filler. There are numerous wood filler products on the market that are usable with pine. You will want to use white or natural color fillers.

Be certain to read the product label on the wood filler you select. The nature of wood fillers requires that you overfill holes or cracks. As the product dries, it tends to shrink. After the product is totally dry, you must sand areas that you have filled. Sand the area flush to the wood's surface. Be careful that you sand with the wood grain.

Although areas holding wood filler can be stained, their final appearance is inevitably different from the actual wood. You can distinguish areas that have been packed with filler. In most instances, the difference in appearance is not all that critical. I would advise, however, that you minimize the use of fillers, especially on exposed and highly visible surfaces.

If you prefer an excellent homemade filler, use pine sawdust and white glue. Squeeze a portion of white glue onto a scrap board and stir sawdust into the glue. Stir the mixture until it is a paste, saturated with the sawdust. Force the paste into nail holes or cracks and allow to dry. As with other fillers, it is best to overfill the areas because there is a certain amount of shrinkage when the glue dries.

This type of homemade filler tends to be less conspicuous than some of the commercial fillers. If you use sufficient sawdust, it will stain almost the same as the actual board. Be certain to sand the filler flush to the board's surface.

Another important preliminary, especially if you plan to stain the project, is to remove any excess wood glue from the surfaces. Stain or oil finishes will not penetrate through any dried glue on the wood. Also, closely examine joints and other areas where you used wood glue. If you find dried glue, remove it using 100-grit abrasive paper. Sand with the grain. In some instances, you might need to use a knife to chip away excess glue.

You also must remove sanding dust from all areas of the project before you apply any finishing product. As mentioned earlier, the ideal tool for this procedure is an air compressor and air gun. An effective alternative is to wipe all surfaces with a clean, dry rag. Remove as much dust and other debris as possible. Dampen a portion of another rag with turpentine and go over all surfaces to remove any remaining dust. Another effective tool for removing dust from a project is a shop vacuum.

An important preliminary activity to finishing is to decide on where to actually do the finishing. The ideal area to do finishing is outside, preferably in a grassy area. The backyard usually has a minimum of dust and a maximum of needed ventilation.

If you must do finishing in the garage or basement, be certain that the area is adequately ventilated. Many finishing products are damaging when inhaled. Most are flammable. Some product vapors can actually be explosive. Do not do any finishing where there is a pilot light or some other type of flame present. Read the label cautions carefully and abide by them. Finishing can be a highly dangerous process. By all means, wear the appropriate breathing device when noted.

TYPES OF FINISHES

Stains. Pine or country projects are generally stained with one of the many colors currently available. As suggested earlier, selecting the appropriate color can be a major task. Stains are usually available with either an oil or water base. My preference is to use an oil-based stain.

If you prefer a light, honey-colored or scrubbed-pine look, one of the maple-colored stains is a good choice. As with all stains, there is considerable variability of colors between manufacturers. You will need to experiment with the various products to find one that you prefer.

I stain most of my pine projects dark. The darker stains tend to blend in with most room decors. I use a Danish walnut color and darken it with a lamp black universal colorant. You might prefer the stain as it comes from the can. Most paint or hardware stores stock a variety of universal colorants that are compatible with oil-based stains. You might want to try them.

After stirring the stain, add a few small squirts of colorant. Mix the colorant into the stain and then test it on a piece of scrap. If it is still not the desired shade, add more colorant. You can, of course, be a bit more scientific and use a measuring device. You also might want to record the amount of colorant you added for future reference.

Surface Finishes. Although projects can be used with only stain applied to them, the wood is not well protected or very attractive. In most instances, you will want to apply either a surface finish or an oil finish.

As with stains and paints, there is an endless array of surface finishing products on the market. Without some prior knowledge, it is almost overwhelming to be confronted with the diversity of products. In addition to the many varnishes available, there are numerous polyurethanes that can be effectively used on pine.

It is worth noting that many of my pine projects are not stained. Numerous project pictures present items that were finished with either lacquer or oil only. My preference is not to use stain on pine and, instead, finish it with a clear lacquer and paste wax. Pine is beautiful with only a lacquer finish. The issue is whether or not it will blend with a particular room decor.

I have used Deft, a clear lacquer, for many years on both pine and hardwood projects. Unlike most varnishes and polyurethanes, lacquers dry very quickly. They are ideal for finishing when you do not have a dust-free environment. Lacquers can be used on stained or unfinished pine with equally good results. If a water-resistant finish is desired, simply increase the number of coats applied. As with all finishing products, read the directions.

Oil Finishes. For an oil finish, I use Watco Danish Oil Finish. Unlike surface finishes, oil finishes are absorbed into the wood. There are numerous other excellent oil finishes on the market that can be used on either stained or unfinished pine. For an inexpensive oil finish, use boiled linseed oil. An oil finish on a pine project, whether stained or not, is extremely attractive.

There are numerous oil finishes that can be used on cutting boards, bowls, or other projects that are to be used with food. Any finishing product that is used on these types of projects should be nontoxic. Watco Danish Oil Finish can be used because it is nontoxic when dry. I use mineral oil on cutting boards and spoons. A good procedure is to warm the wood and rub the oil into it. Use several treatments. Vegetable oil is not recommended. In some instances, your own experience might give you the preferable way to finish projects that will be used with food.

Paints. The use of paints, either oil based or latex, is another way to finish your projects. Although my preference is to use latex, you might prefer the oil paints. As with stain, the range of colors can be very confusing. You might prefer to use colors already present in your house. There is also a selection of Early American colors available from several mail-order suppliers. Pine accepts paint very well, and you might want to consider its use on a number of your projects.

FINISHING PROCEDURES

Although you will develop your own procedures to finish pine projects, it seems appropriate to detail how I do it. I am confident there are better and more effective methods; however, the following procedures have worked well for me.

Whenever I am finishing, I spread several layers of newspaper on the surface where I will be working. In that I am somewhat careless when applying stain, the paper is critical. In addition to newspaper, I have several scraps of pine available on which the freshly stained project can be placed to dry. If you leave the stained piece on the newspapers, the newsprint will come off and be absorbed by the wood.

Be certain your finishing area is well ventilated if you are not doing the work outside. You might want to use one of the various masks that filter toxic fumes. If you are using an oil-based stain, you also might want to wear rubber or plastic gloves. I generally use surgical gloves, which are thicker and stronger than the ones available in paint stores. Gloves prevent the stain from getting all over your hands. They also eliminate the need to use turpentine or other stain removers on your skin.

For applying the stain, I use either a 1- or 2-inch-wide brush. As a rule, I purchase inexpensive brushes and then throw them away when the project is done. I have found that with stain, the type and quality of the brush is not all that critical. You also can use a rag for applying the stain. Use a rag that is not loaded with lint. You do not want fabric remains all over your project.

When you are applying the stain with a brush, simply spread it around on the project's various surfaces. I tend to use a lot of stain and really slop it on the wood. The amount of stain used does not affect the color of the project. More does not make it darker. Be certain all the surfaces are adequately covered. You do not need to worry about brush marks with stain.

I usually stain the back portion of the project first. If it is a cabinet, I do the inside first. It is best to simply pick up the project and spread the stain. Make the process as simple as possible. Wear an apron or old clothes so you can hold the piece in your lap while you are spreading the stain.

Areas on the project that have end grain I stain last. End grain on the wood tends to absorb stain like a sponge. As a result, they often are somewhat darker in appearance. To adequately cover the end-grain areas, you often need to force stain in with the brush. There is little you can do to prevent the end grain from absorbing the stain. It is the nature of pine to be porous.

When the entire project is covered with stain, I place it on the wood scraps for a few minutes. Usually the label directions will indicate how long you should allow the stain to dry. I begin wiping the stain off while it is still wet. If you allow the stain to dry totally, the surface will be blotchy looking. You can always restain the project if necessary.

Use lint-free rags to wipe off the stain. I tend to rub the surface lightly as I wipe off the stain. Wipe with the wood grain. Do not press or rub too hard, or you will remove all the stain. Fold a portion of the rag to get into the various corners of the project. You want all the excess stain removed. When wiping is complete, place the project on scraps and allow it to dry thoroughly. Drying time varies depending upon the product, temperature, and humidity. Generally, the label directions will indicate a time frame for proper drying.

Because rags and newspaper used in finishing can combust spontaneously, you should dispose of them immediately. If you cannot burn them, spread them outside until you can dispose of them properly. By all means, do not roll them into a ball and toss them in a corner. These procedures also apply to the clothes you were wearing if they are covered with stain.

When the stain is dry, I apply a surface finish to the project. As indicated, I prefer using Deft, a high-quality lacquer. When preparing to apply the lacquer, I again spread newspaper and use scraps of wood. I recommend that you wear an appropriate breathing device when you are using lacquer.

Since lacquers dry very quickly, they are ideal for the hobbyist finisher. They can be used in the kinds of areas most people do their finishing. My shop is in the garage and it is a perpetual mess. It is by no means a dust-free environment. I have found that Deft usually dries before it can begin attracting too much dust. As always, read the directions on the product before you use it.

Although there are many high-quality brushes available for use with lacquers, I generally purchase the most inexpensive. Lacquer spreads easily and brush marks are generally not a problem. You will find that the cheaper brushes tend to lose a few bristles during use. I simply pick them off the surface and brush over the area. Rather than clean the brush when finished, I simply discard it.

You can use lacquer thinner to clean brushes if you prefer. It also will clean lacquer from your hands. This product is also dangerous and should be used according to label directions.

Few projects lend themselves to being lacquered entirely in one step. Normally you will need to finish a portion of the project at a time. As a rule, I finish the exposed areas first. For example, on a mirror, I finish the front surface and the edges first. When these are done, I finish the back surface. This type of procedure varies from project to project.

As with stain, the end grain tends to absorb the lacquer very quickly. You will need to spread additional coats on the various end-grain areas of the project. It is almost impossible to totally fill the end grain with lacquer.

As a rule, I put three to four coats of Deft on most projects. For pieces that will be used in the bathroom or around moisture, I put on additional coats. You would be well advised to consult the label directions for projects that will be exposed to water and other liquids.

When the lacquer is dry, I go over all surfaces with (0000) steel wool. The steel wool removes any dust particles that have stuck to the surface. It also cuts the gloss of the lacquer and makes its appearance somewhat dull. Steel wool greatly enhances the final finish. Depending upon the project, I sometimes use steel wool between coats of lacquer. Do not rub too hard or you will cut through the finish with the wool. Do not use steel wool on end grain because the grain tends to pull out hairs that attach themselves to the wood. Using a rag or air gun, remove all the strands of steel wool left on the project's surface.

As a final procedure, I rub all surfaces, except the end grain, with paste wax. There are numerous excellent paste waxes on the market. I use clear Trewax paste wax, clear Butcher's Wax paste wax, or Johnson's paste wax. Read the label directions on the can and use accordingly. These are excellent waxes to use on your projects on an ongoing basis. They are especially useful for projects used in the bathroom or where moisture is present. Incidentally, flannel rags are very effective for polishing the waxed surfaces.

FINISHING MIRRORS

After you have finished a mirror frame, glue the mirror into the frame using white glue. Do not spread wax in the recessed mirror area or the glue will not hold. Apply the glue between the edge of the mirror and the recessed area of the frame. Then cover the back of the mirror and the recessed area with a piece of construction paper. Measure and cut the paper to the needed dimensions. Spread white glue on the edge of the paper and press in place. For procedures on cutting mirror glass, refer to Project 11.

HANGING DEVICES AND PROCEDURES

With few exceptions, the process of hanging your wood projects is not a matter of concern until you are completely done with the finishing process. You prepared some pieces for hanging during the crafting process. For example, you drilled hanging holes through the support pieces of shelves. You might or might not want to use these holes to hang your items after exploring some other options for hanging projects.

The major consideration in hanging your projects is the kind of walls you have in your house or apartment. Another variable that affects hanging is whether or not you want to be able to remove your wood pieces if and when you move. Related to this issue, if you are an apartment dweller, are any restrictions you have on how you can hang things on the walls. I will deal with some of these concerns in hanging projects and also a few tips on patching holes.

Most new housing construction has what is generally called *drywall construction*. Simply stated, this usually means that your walls are a kind of plaster board that does not lend itself to simply hanging something with a nail. This is the kind of wall that tends to crumble when you try to hang something on it. Drywall usually has a paper kind of surface and is anywhere from ½ to ¾ inch thick. This type of wall material makes for great housing, but is lousy stuff for trying to hang things.

The other kind of walls, frequently found in older homes, are plaster walls. These walls are usually very hard and thick, and when you drive a nail into them, the plaster tends to fall away around the nail. The wall tends to powder and chip when you try to drive a nail into it. Plaster walls can be miserable things on which to hang anything. Incidentally, if you do want to drive a nail into a plaster wall, place a piece of transparent tape over the spot where the nail is to be driven. The tape tends to hold the plaster material in place and thus support the nail.

One piece of information that might or might not prove helpful in hanging things is to remember that usually 2-x-4 studs are behind the walls. Most new construction has a stud every 16 inches, while older homes are often built with 20 inches or more space between the studs. If you are lucky enough to have studs in the approximate area where you want to hang something, you might want to use them. They can be especially useful when you are hanging a shelf that will carry a considerable amount of weight.

Frequently, you can locate the studs—on drywall construction at least—by looking for small indentations in the wall's surface. They generally run from the floor to the ceiling. These little pot marks are where the plasterboard was nailed to the stud. Each one represents a nail head that was not patched over very well.

You also can buy a *stud finder* to use in locating the studs in the walls. Essentially, a stud finder is a small magnet that elevates a red pointer when contact is made over the head of a nail. I have not been overly successful in finding studs with these devices.

Normally, when I need to locate a stud for hanging something, I find myself looking for nail holes and tapping the wall with a knuckle. The sound of the wall when a stud is present is distinctly different from the hollow sound between studs. To confirm the stud, using a small finishing nail, I punch a hole through the wall. Usually these procedures will result in locating a stud for hanging items. You then can measure from this stud to locate other studs that you might need.

You can fill holes in the wall easily with either spackling paste or patching compound. This material is like putty and usually is white in color. If you have painted walls, you can mix a little paint into some of the spackling paste before you fill the hole. This kind of material is excellent for patching nail holes that remain when you remove items from the wall. As always, read the directions on the can prior to using.

I have found that the easiest way to hang wood items when screws or nails cannot be driven into studs is to use brass hangers and picture hooks (Fig. 4-1). Both of these items are generally available at local hardware stores or from mail-order suppliers. Screw the brass hangers on the back of the project with the round top extending above the surface. Figure 4-2 depicts how the hangers appear when placed on the back of a shelf. The picture hooks slide through the hanger holes and hold the unit to the wall.

Fig. 4-1. Brass hangers and picture hooks.

To hang a shelf using these devices, place the unit against the wall at the exact location desired. Use a small torpedo level, placed on the shelf top's

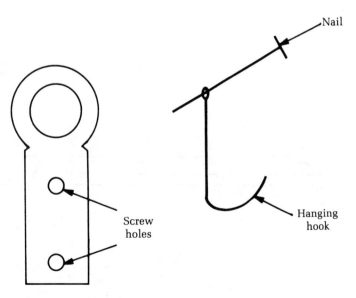

Nail

Screw holes

Hanging hook

surface, to level the unit. Move one end of the shelf up and down until the bubble in the level vial is between the two lines, indicating that the shelf is level. Using a pencil, mark the wall at the top edge of both brass hangers. These two points are where you need to drive the picture hooks into the wall. As the devices indicate, the picture-hook nails need to be driven into the wall at an angle.

Another type of hanging device that is especially effective for shelves is a keyhole mounting plate (Fig. 4-3). Unlike the brass hangers and picture hooks, when these devices are routed and secured in place on the back surfaces of shelf legs, they cannot be seen. The keyholes in the plates are designed to slide over the head of a screw or nail that penetrates a wall or wood surface, thus preventing the shelf from sliding off the nails or screws.

An effective device to use with the keyhole-mounting plate, especially on drywall construction, is a Molly bolt or Molly jack nut. Locate a pack of them in a hardware store and read the directions on the package. Molly bolts come in various lengths. Once secured to the wall, only the actual holding bolt can be removed. Part of the device remains permanently secured in the wall. Molly bolts are excellent devices for hanging projects, but do require a bit more time, tools, and accuracy. Incidentally, Molly bolts are also excellent devices if you want to hang a project on an inside, hollow-core door.

For placement of the keyhole plates on the legs of a shelf, you need to rout a ⅝-inch-wide trench that is approximately 1⅝ inches long. The length of the trench is determined by the actual length of the plate. Rout the trench to a depth of at least ³⁄₁₆ inch. If you have used a support piece in the shelf design, the routed area should be below it. If you have not used a support piece, rout the trenches near the top edge of the legs (Fig. 4-4). You also can

Fig. 4-2. Brass hangers on a shelf.

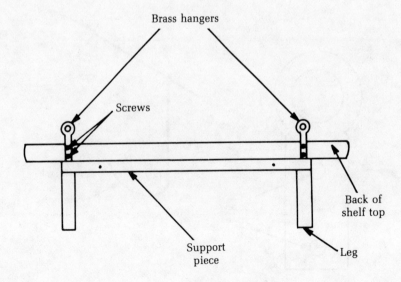

Brass hangers

Screws

Back of shelf top

Support piece

Leg

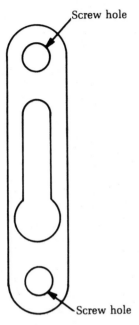

Screw hole

Screw hole

Fig. 4-3. Keyhole
mounting plate.

rout the trench beginning in the back edge of the shelf top and extending down into the leg.

The trench is best routed using a ⅝-inch-diameter straight router bit on a table-mounted router. A properly aligned fence is mandatory for routing the two trenches. After the routing is complete, drill two ⅜-inch holes in each trench. The holes should overlap each other. The drilled holes allow the head of the screw or nail to penetrate through the plate and into the leg. Using ½-×-5-inch flat-head wood screws, secure the plates into the trenches.

Another hanging device that is effective with mirrors or other small projects is the sawtooth hanger (Fig. 4-5). Center the sawtooth at the top back of a project and secure it in place with two small brads. Then place the sawtooth on a nail or screw in the wall or other surface. You can make the project hang straight by placing the proper tooth area over the nail. These devices are available in a range of lengths and are inexpensive. You can obtain them from most hardware stores or mail-order suppliers.

For small mirrors and sometimes even T Shelves, you can use a small, brass picture hanger and *escutcheon pins* (Fig. 4-6). Escutcheon pins are simply small brass brads with a round head. They are available in a range of lengths and diameters. These smaller hangers should be used only on projects that are not too heavy. They are excellent for hanging small mirrors or similar projects.

On occasion, you might want to use decorative ring hangers on mirrors

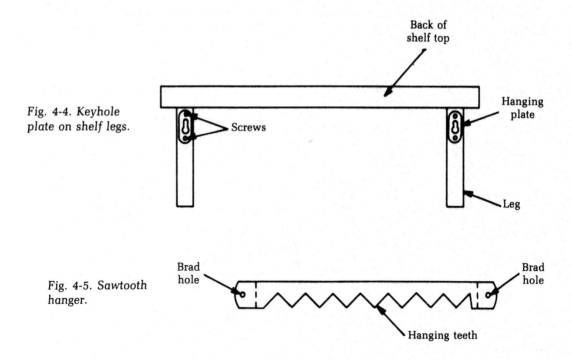

Fig. 4-4. Keyhole
plate on shelf legs.

Back of
shelf top

Hanging
plate

Screws

Leg

Fig. 4-5. Sawtooth
hanger.

Brad
hole

Brad
hole

Hanging teeth

or other small projects. Center the hanger on the top edge of a frame and screw it in place (Fig. 4-7). After the ring is in place on the project, hang it on a nail extending from the wall or other surface. The nail needs to extend far enough from the wall so that the ring can fit over its head. There is a large variety of this type of hanger on the market, and usually they are available in various sizes at local hardware or discount stores.

Another device with which I have had some success is a keyhole router bit (Fig. 4-8). The bit allows you to rout a keyhole in the back surface of a project. As with the keyhole plate hanger, you simply slip the slot over a nail or screw head and it is secured in place. When the bit is set for a ⅜-inch depth of cut, it makes the slot as it moves forward in the wood. You will want to hold the router and make the rout freehand with this bit. The procedure takes some practice, but the keyhole router bit is an effective device for preparing projects for hanging.

Although not a device as such, double-faced tape also can be used to hang projects. Usually the tape is available in either rolls or small squares. As its name implies, it is sticky on both surfaces. Place a small strip or square of tape onto the back surface of the project. Remove the protective covering from the other surface and set the project in place. The tape bond is very strong when in place, especially on smooth surfaces. You will find, however, that the tape can remove paint when you pull it off a surface.

As you are confronted with the task of hanging your small pine projects, you will find that there are other devices and techniques for hanging them. I try to browse in hardware stores or review catalogs looking for new and more effective ways to hang projects. It is an excellent way to learn more about what is available to do a job that no one particularly enjoys.

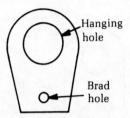

Fig. 4-6. Small brass hanger.

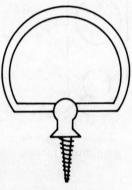

Fig. 4-7. Decorative ring hanger.

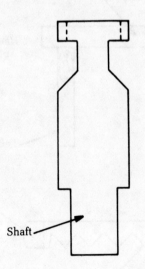

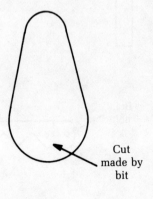

Fig. 4-8. Keyhole router bit.

Appendix:

Suppliers and Magazines

MAIL-ORDER SUPPLIERS

The following list of mail-order suppliers is but a sampling of companies that specialize in crafting supplies, woodworking tools, and related accessories. Each company has a mail-order catalog and, in some instances, a toll-free telephone number to facilitate your ordering. While some companies provide free mail-order catalogs, others have a moderate charge. It is best to write the company and request information on its catalog.

Constantine
2050 Eastchester Road
Bronx, NY 10461

Craftsman
1735 W. Cortland Ct.
Addison, IL 60101

The Fine Tool Shops, Inc.
20 Backus Ave.
P.O. Box 1262
Danbury, CT 06810

Frog Tool Co., Ltd.
P.O. Box 8325
Chicago, IL 60680

Highland Hardware
1045 N. Highland Ave., NE
Atlanta, GA 30306

Hiller Hardware Co.
P.O. Box 1762
Columbia, SC 29202

Woodcraft
41 Atlantic Ave.
P.O. Box 4000
Woburn, MA 01888

The Woodworkers' Store
21801 Industrial Blvd.
Rogers, MN 55374

Klockit
P.O. Box 629
Lake Geneva, WI 53147

Meisel Hardware Specialties
P.O. Box 258
Mound, MN 55364

Sears, Roebuck and Co.
Sears Tower
Chicago, IL 60684

Seven Corners Ace Hardware, Inc.
216 West 7th St.
St. Paul, MN 55102

Trend-Lines
375 Beacham St.
P.O. Box 6447
Chelsea, MA 02150

Warren Tool Co., Inc.
Rt. 1, P.O. Box 14
Rhinebeck, NY 12572

Woodworkers Supply of New Mexico
5604 Alameda, NE
Albuquerque, NM 87113

Woodworks
4013-A Clay Ave.
Ft. Worth, TX 76117

WOODWORKING MAGAZINES

The following list of magazines is for those interested in all facets of woodworking. For subscription information, write to the addresses given.

The American Woodworker
P.O. Box 1408
Hendersonville, TN 37077

Fine Woodworking
The Taunton Press, Inc.
P.O. Box 355
Newton, CT 06470

The Mallet
National Carvers Museum Foundation
14960 Woodcarver Rd.
Monument, CO 80132

Wood
Better Homes and Gardens
P.O. Box 10693
Des Moines, IA 50380

Bibliography

Berry, James B. *Wood Identification*. New York: Dover Publications, Inc., 1966.

Clifford, Jerrold R. *Basic Woodworking and Carpentry*. Blue Ridge Summit, PA.: TAB BOOKS, Inc., 1980.

Constantine, Albert Jr. *Know Your Woods*. New York: Charles Scribner's Sons, 1959.

Daniele, Joseph. *Building Early American Furniture*. Harrisburg, PA.: Stackpole Books, 1974.

Edlin, Herbert L. *What Wood Is That?* New York: The Viking Press, 1969.

Fraser, B. Kay. *Tole Painting*. New York: Sterling, 1971.

Groneman, Chris H. *General Woodworking*. New York: McGraw-Hill Book Co., 1971.

Harrar, E.S. *Hough's Encyclopedia of American Woods*. 13 volumes. New York: Robert Speller and Sons, 1957.

Hauser, Priscilla. *Tole and Decorative Painting*. New York: Van Nostrand Reinhold Co., 1977.

Howard, Joyce. *New Tole and Folk Art Designs*. Radnor, PA.: Chilton Book Co., 1979.

Kellell, Russell H. *The Pine Furniture of Early New England*. New York: Dover Publications, Inc., 1956.

Midkiff, Pat. *The Complete Book of Stenciling*. New York: Sterling, 1978.

Pain, F. *The Practical Wood Turner*. New York: Drake Publishers, Inc., 1974.

Schiffer, Nancy and Herbert. *Woods We Live With*. Exton, PA.: Schiffer Publishing, Ltd., 1977.

Sloane, Eric. *Reverence for Wood*. New York: Ballantine Books, 1965.

Tangerman, E.J. *Whittling and Woodcarving*. New York: Dover Publications, Inc., 1936.

Index

Other Bestsellers From TAB

☐ **MAKING MOVABLE WOODEN TOYS—Alan and Gill Bridgewater**

This book contains 20 toy projects that will challenge and excite the creative woodworker in you. Fro Russian nesting dolls to an American folk art baby rattle, traditional pull-along toys to English soldiers, these are the toys adults enjoy making and children enjoy playing with! The designs employ whittling and lathe work among other techniques. Precise, over-the-shoulder instructions and numerous work-in-progress illustrations guide you through every step of construction. 240 pp., 106 illus., 7 × 10

Paper $18.95   **Hard $23.95**
Book No. 3079

☐ **DESIGNING AND BUILDING CHILDRENS' FURNITURE, WITH 61 PROJECTS—2nd Edition—Percy W. Blandford**

This book provides complete detail in measuring, marking, designing, building, and finishing child-size furniture. Projects include a baby's playpen, chest of drawers, safety gate, toy box, painting easel, rocking horse, and more. Percy W. Blandford is a recognized authority in woodworking and other practical crafts. His superb line drawings illustrate this step-by-step guide. 192 pp., Over 150 illus.

Paper $17.95   **Hard $21.95**
Book No. 3064

☐ **MAKING ANTIQUE FURNITURE—Edited by Vic Taylor**

A collection of some of the finest furniture ever made is found within the pages of this project book designed for the intermediate- to advanced-level craftsman. Reproducing European period furniture pieces such as a Windsor chair, a Jacobean box stool, a Regency table, a Sheraton writing desk, a Lyre-end occasional table, and many traditional furnishings is sure to provide you with pleasure and satisfaction. Forty projects include materials lists and step-by-step instructions. 160 pp., Fully illustrated, 8 1/2″ × 11″

Paper $19.95   **Hard $25.95**
Book No. 3056

☐ **WOODWORKER'S 30 BEST PROJECTS—Editors of** *Woodworker* **Magazine**

A collection of some of the finest furniture ever made can be found within the pages of this project book. Designed for the woodworker who has already mastered the basics, the projects presented in this book are for the intermediate- to advanced-level craftsman. Each furniture project comes complete with detailed instructions, a materials list, exploded views of working diagrams, a series of step-by-step, black-and-white photos, and a photograph of the finished piece. 224 pp., 300 illus.

Paper $18.95   **Hard $23.95**
Book No. 3021

☐ **DESIGNING AND BUILDING SPACE-SAVING FURNITURE, WITH 28 PROJECTS—2nd Edition—Percy W. Blandford**

Step-by-step directions, exploded diagrams and two-color illustrations are included with detailed advice on planning and preparing, measuring, woodworking techniques, fasteners, upholstery, and tool usage. Author Percy Blandford is an internationally recognized master craftsman. He has been writing about the how-tos of woodworking since 1940. In this book, he provides a wealth of easy-to-accomplish projects for increasing storage space in every room in your home. 192 pp., 200 illus.2-color throughout

Paper $17.95   **$21.95**
Book No. 3074

☐ **101 OUTSTANDING WOODEN TOYS AND CHILDRENS' FURNITURE PROJECTS—Wayne L. Kadar**

Turn inexpensive materials into fun and functional toys. Challenge and charm the youngsters in your life with building blocks, pull toys, shape puzzles, stilts, trains, trucks, boats, planes, dolls and more. This step-by-step guide is abundantly illustrated and provides complete materials lists. 304 pp., 329 illus.

Paper $19.95   **Hard $24.95**
Book No. 3058

☐ **BUILD YOUR OWN GRANDFATHER CLOCK AND SAVE—John A. Nelson**

Thorough and exact plans make this challenging project achievable by woodworkers of all skill levels. The design is an adaptation of two or three clocks made by 18th-century clockmaker Nathaniel Mulliken. Every aspect of construction is covered, from building the case and hood to installing premade movements. Nelson even details how to make your own brass hinges and escutcheons from scratch. Many illustrations complement the step-by-step instructions. 144 pp., 99 illus.

Paper $15.95   **Hard $19.95**
Book No. 3053

☐ **DESIGNING AND BUILDING COLONIAL AND EARLY AMERICAN FURNITURE, WITH 47 PROJECTS—2nd Edition—Percy W. Blandford**

Original designs that allow plenty of room for creativity! This volume captures the spirit and challenge of authentic Early American and Colonial craftsmanship. Blandford, an internationally recognized expert in the field, provides first-rate illustrations and simple instructions on the art of reproducing fine furniture. Every project in this volume is an exquisite reproduction of centuries-old originals: drop-leaf tables, peasant chairs, swivel-top tables, firehouse armchair, ladderback chairs, tilt-top box tables, hexagonal candle stands, trestle dining tables, wagon seat benches, jackstands, dry sinks, love seats, and Welsh dressers. 192 pp., 188 illus.

Paper $15.95   **Hard $21.95**
Book No. 3014

Other Bestsellers From TAB